BUSTED

A Handbook for Lawyers and Their Clients

BUSTED

A Handbook for
Lawyers and Their Clients
with reference to the new
Criminal Procedure Law

by
OLIVER A. ROSENGART

St. Martin's Press · New York

St. Martin's Press
175 Fifth Avenue
New York, N.Y. 10010

AFFILIATED PUBLISHERS: Macmillan & Company, Limited, London
—also at Bombay, Calcutta, Madras and Melbourne
—the Macmillan Company of Canada, Limited, Toronto.

To all the men and women in cages.

CONTENTS

PREFACE

The criminal courts are political institutions. They reflect in kind many of the inequities and hypocrisies of our society as a whole. The courts enforce laws that are politically made, and they maintain the status quo against forces seeking change. The courts mirror and perpetuate racism in that the vast majority of judges are white even though the defendants in any urban area are overwhelmingly black or of Spanish descent; the courts discriminate against the poor who are not able to post even low bail, or afford a lawyer, and who face alien middle-class standards in sentencing. The alcoholic, the drug addict, the psychologically troubled, the rebellious, the political activist, and those on the fringes of society are dealt with the only way the court knows how: repressively. The visitor to the court instinctively recognizes its partisan nature, if perhaps only through the symbol of pomposity which enshrouds the man sitting up front in black robes. To the defendant, however, the political nature of the criminal court is more real and more damaging. He or she has no choice but to play the game of criminal justice . . . a game in which the defendant has had no part in making the rules.

The lawyer is the person called upon to pull the levers for the defendant who is not supposed to, and rarely does, understand the rituals and technicalities of the criminal process. Generally, the defendant expects the lawyer to use his special skills to exploit whatever can be gained from the normal functioning of the criminal system. Of course, defendants are not always convicted. The procedural safeguards embodied in the concept of "due process" are occasionally utilized to secure dismissals or acquittals, and a lawyer acts irresponsibly when he or she is not thoroughly familiar with the law and practice surrounding these and other techniques. The ineluctable fact remains, however, that the criminal law works best for those already advantaged or privileged.

In those cases where it is not only the court that is political, but the defendant as well, the underlying political conflict may surface in the courtroom in what is known as the political trial. Indeed we can see today a rising incidence of such trials as the open antagonisms of the political forces in America intensify. In the political trial the defendant makes a choice to take the matter one step behind the legal issues, for example the racism or repression that placed the defendant before the court in the first place. Here the lawyer is called upon to be more than a technician; he or she is asked to be a political organizer of the courtroom. Perhaps even more so in the political trial, the lawyer must be the master of his legal skills, for these skills are the tools of the defendant who has chosen to challenge and expose the political repressiveness of the court.

A transparent illusion of fairness is fostered by the lawyer's ability to utilize his knowledge of the criminal court system and its machinations often to the benefit of his client. The function of the lawyer is to provide experience and judgment rather than intellect in the criminal courts; the important decisions are not usually those of law or legal theory, but rather when to adjourn a case, when to plead guilty, which judge to appear before, etc.

What is perhaps most important for a lawyer, however, at least in a political sense, is perspective—not the perspective born of callousness or insensitivity, a "win some, lose some" attitude—but rather the perspective of the relative incompleteness or inadequacy of the legal solution. We use "relative" because to the individual defendant acquittal or dismissal on the one hand or conviction and jail sentence on the other is of paramount significance. In societal terms, however, successfully defending a person against criminal charges and returning the defendant to the street raises the question of what the street has to offer that person. More often than not it is only further oppression, racism, and poverty. It is important for lawyers to remember that currently the only solution they offer is that of a short-run soporific. The solution required calls for much more.

What Ollie Rosengart's book describes in lucid detail is the practical workings of the New York criminal courts. It cuts through the facade to portray the many parts in their workaday operation in the ordinary as well as political case. It has been a special concern of ours that the author set down this accumulation of information and experience to share with others about to practice in the criminal courts. During the past several years the New York Chapter of the National Lawyers Guild has assumed as one of its primary tasks the role of providing lawyers for those arrested in the course of their many and varied political activities. This book sets out the basic text with which the lawyer can proceed into any area of the criminal court system.

Although the book is keyed to the criminal courts of New York City, one suspects that criminal practice on the misdemeanor level is not dissimilar in any of the large urban centers of the United States. What is even more certain, however, is that the oppressiveness of the New York Criminal Courts parallels closely that of criminal courts throughout the country. If you are poor, non-white, or political, you will face the full brunt of racism and repression that characterizes criminal courts everywhere.

September 28, 1970   National Lawyers Guild

INTRODUCTION

For over two years, until July, 1970 I was a staff attorney with Mobilization For Youth Legal Services, on New York's Lower East Side, doing only criminal law. During that time I was privileged to handle cases as diverse as the neighborhood, from drugs to homicides, and street demonstrations to riots. The experience taught me a great deal both about the police, court, and penal institutions of New York, and about what it takes to be a good criminal lawyer. The first requirement is a thorough knowledge of the workings of the criminal court, including the judges, D.A.'s, plea bargaining, the kinds of cases that can win at trial, sentencing practices, the effect of participation in programs, the effect of delay, and so on. Secondly, a lawyer must of course have a familiarity with criminal law, but the field is small and finite and not difficult to understand. In the vast majority of cases, the material taught in law school has no relevance and the lawyer need only know the penal law, the procedural rules, exclusionary rules (search and seizure, confessions, etc.) and the rules of evidence. Thirdly, and probably most important, a criminal lawyer must have a feel for human behavior (particularly his client's), and a knowledge of what life in the streets is like, or, simply stated, good common sense. All of the above, except common sense, is fairly easily mastered and this book is meant to be an introductory guide to those who want to try. The book is also, I believe, fully understandable by non-lawyers and is meant for anyone who wants to remove the mystique from the Criminal Court.

The reader should keep in mind that this book is meant to be nothing more than an introductory guide to practice in the Criminal Court. It contains a fairly complete account of the practices and procedures of the Criminal Court, but the newcomer will not have a true feeling for the course of a case until he or she practices or observes for a while. It also contains an introduction to the various areas of the law (with the exception of the law of evidence) that the reader should know, with a few case citations. However, when it comes time to write a brief, this book can do nothing more than serve as a starting point for thinking and research. I have tried only to summarize the law in several areas and give a few examples of fact patterns that appear frequently, together with possible ways of handling them. The reader should also keep in mind that this book deals only with the Criminal Court, which handles misdemeanors, felonies which are reduced to misdemeanors, and felonies up until indictment. It does not cover the handling of felonies in Supreme Court, which, incidentally, do not go to trial in over 90% of the cases.

The price of the book was set at the lowest level which would insure meeting the cost of printing. It is relatively high because of the limited audience to which the book is directed. Profits, if any, will go to the National Lawyers Guild and other Movement organizations. If any individual or organization cannot afford the price, call or write the Guild and a free copy will be sent.

Finally, I would like to take this opportunity to express a few personal thoughts about what it is like to practice in the Criminal Court. Fear, horror, shock, surprise, anger and frustration were a few of my emotions when I started working in the court. For any lawyer it is at first a frightening and nerve-wracking place to work in, primarily because of the enormous pressure and responsibility, but, of course, it becomes easier with experience. The omnipresent human suffering in the building makes it a hard place for sensitive people to take, and it isn't the sensitive people who are crazy. Family and friends can be seen waiting for hours and occasionally crying and the barbaric correctional system permeates the building, shepherding human beings to and from cages, sometimes bound in handcuffs. Every so often a defendant loses his temper at the injustice of being caged and hollers at everyone, with the result that he is quickly put back into a cage and often ordered to undergo a psychiatric examination. It is also startling, for anyone who has worked with or gotten to know defendants on a personal level, to see how ignorant the court and penal institutions are of their behavior. Judges, often well-meaning, can be heard lecturing youngsters on the dangers of heroin, and human beings are supposed to solve their difficulties in coping with the horrible conditions of their society by spending time in jail. It is surprising to find that there are people, even intelligent ones, that still believe in the system. Frustration is another often-felt emotion among defense lawyers, although things should get better now that jury trials are available for misdemeanors. In trials before judges there are almost no acquittals in police-brutality cases and even in ordinary cases judges generally accept even the most blatantly obvious untruths from police officers. It is terribly frustrating to try a case when you believe your client is innocent, the police officer is obviously lying, and you know beforehand that your client will be convicted of at least a violation.

On the positive side, the court is terribly overcrowded, inefficient and slow-moving, which is generally to the defendant's advantage. Delay often means that police officers and complainants fail to appear and cases are dismissed for lack of prosecution, and, for the defendant in jail, overcrowded calendars usually mean better plea offers. A long delay often results in a case being settled by a very low plea or a non-jail sentence. The slow pace at which a case moves works to the disadvantage of only the innocent who are in jail and, if a lawyer pushes a case, delays in misdemeanor cases can usually be avoided. Also on the positive side, there are several fairly progressive judges on the bench and sometimes a case can be maneuvered so that sentence is imposed by one of these men. In addition, many judges realize the futility of jail and will bend over backwards to give a break to a man who is in a program or who shows that he has changed the pattern of his life. Keeping that fact in mind, and helping your client get into a program or, in some cases, helping him find a meaningful job, can achieve remarkable results in the court.

Although this book is based on my experience as a defense lawyer in New York City, I believe it is of value to anyone who wants to learn about the criminal court process of any city. The basic procedural aspects of a criminal case are essentially the same in almost all courts; that is, every case goes from arrest to arraignment, to preliminary hearing (which might have a different name), to hearings on motions, to trial and then sentencing. The tactical advice on how to conduct arraignments, interview clients, talk to witnesses, discover the prosecutor's case, conduct preliminary hearings, etc., is basically applicable everywhere. The material on motion practice, which contains both law and suggested ways of handling typical fact-patterns, needs little adaptation since most of the case law comes from the Supreme Court and is based on the U.S. Constitution, which of course applies everywhere, and also since the ways in which arrests and searches take place are pretty much the same everywhere. Similarly, the chapter on trials is almost entirely general and applicable everywhere. The main areas where practices differ from city to city (and often even from county to county) are dismissals through participation in programs, special programs for addicts (if any), and plea bargaining. Although the tactics of plea bargaining described in this book are generally appropriate everywhere, the practices vary enormously and the only way to really learn the plea bargaining system as well as the court's relationship to programs is to hang around the courthouse and talk to the lawyers who work there. In the final analysis this book, or any book, can serve only as an introduction to the criminal court system, and, if the reader wants to completely understand the system, reading must be followed by a substantial amount of observing and talking to people who work in the court.

Chapter 1

THE ARREST

In most cases the crucial time for a lawyer or any other witness to be present is at the time of arrest. Since much of what takes place in court involves disputes over what occurred at the time of arrest, the ideal would be to have a lawyer and a sound movie camera on the scene. Obviously, there are few situations in which a lawyer will be present at the time of arrest. The most common are demonstrations and this chapter is mostly about the role of a lawyer at demonstrations.

A. Peaceful Demonstrations

The most important roles that any lawyer can play at a demonstration are (1) to be a trained evidence gatherer; (2) to inhibit police misconduct; and (3) under certain circumstances, to mediate between the police and demonstrators. Arrests at peaceful demonstrations are often totally unfounded and are followed by fabrications by the arresting officer in court. Frequently an arrestee is assigned to a particular arresting officer because it is that officer's turn to go to court or because the real arresting officer roughed up the arrestee, and the assigned arresting officer never even saw the arrestee before he or she arrived at the police station. Obviously, in such a case, all his testimony in court is made up. In addition to watching unfounded arrests, a lawyer's observations of police attacks on demonstrators are of crucial importance at trials of defendants or at Civilian Complaint Review Board trials on police misconduct.

In order to be an observer at demonstrations, and in order to advise the groups who are demonstrating, the lawyer must of course know the law in this area. An excellent summary is

1

contained in a pamphlet entitled "Demonstration Guidelines," published by the Civil Liberties Defense & Education Fund of the New York Civil Liberties Union, New York, 1970. Publication of "Demonstration Guidelines" was made possible by the George E. Rundquist Memorial Fund, and it is reprinted below in its entirety.

I.
Demonstrations on Public Streets

A. Marches. There are basic rules of thumb for demonstrations, based upon case law, which are fairly easy to follow. It is now clear that a non-violent group of people marching on a public street to make a political point, may not be penalized *if they stay on the sidewalk. No permit is required. A sidewalk march is not a parade.* This means that you can march as far as you like, and string out the line of march as much as necessary. Noise, such as singing and chanting, the stopping of traffic on cross streets, even inconvenience to pedestrians, do not make such a march into a breach of the peace (disorderly conduct). Sections of the disorderly conduct statute, such as that penalizing congregating together and failing to move on when ordered to do so, (PL 240.20 [6]), may seem to cover the case, but the Supreme Court has repeatedly held that such a march on the *sidewalk* of a *public street* is protected. *Cox v. Louisiana*, 379 U.S. 536 (1965); *Gregory v. Chicago*, 22 L.Ed. 2d 134 (1969).

In the street (on the roadway), a march is much harder to defend legally. It may violate traffic regulations, as well as the parade ordinance (N.Y.C. Admin. Code 435-9.0). If such a march is peaceful, *and a parade permit has been refused*, it is probably not a disorderly conduct (*Gregory v. Chicago, supra.*) Operationally however, it is an almost certain arrest situation, because of the snarled traffic. For First Amendment purposes, in short, try to stay out of the roadway or get a parade permit from the Police Department.

It is important to appoint marshals, to try to keep the march within prescribed limits, e.g. on the sidewalk. If possible, some persons, especially photographers or lawyers, should be non-participating observers, to testify, if necessary, that the marchers were peaceful. The status of such observers is protected by the First Amendment and police regulations.

It has been held that the mere fact that hecklers or others opposed to the demonstrators' position are present is not enough to justify the police in arresting a speaker or demonstrators. *Cox v. Louisiana, supra; Rockwell v. Morris*, 211 N.Y.S. 2d 25 (I Dept. 1961) aff. 10 N.Y. 2d 721 (1961).

B. Barricades. The police frequently erect barricades which prevent marchers from getting in front of a desired goal, e.g. the United Nations. Limitations of demonstrations may be justified to keep traffic flowing, but not to keep the demonstrators from reaching their audience. Demonstration organizers should try to negotiate with the police over this. But note that an acquittal of a disorderly conduct charge is possible for violation of unreasonable restrictions. *People v. Solomonow*, 291 N.Y.S. 2d 145 (Crim. Ct. 1968).

C. Speeches. There is a city ordinance still on the books (Ad. Code 435-7) requiring a permit for speeches. It has been held unconstitutional. *Kunz v. New York*, 340 U.S. 290 (1951). You do not need a permit to speak *even if a crowd gathers* and if anyone asks whether you have a permit, say that none is required. Operationally, it is good, however, to keep a space on the sidewalk open for pedestrians. Although this is probably subject to constitutional attack, under present law you should have an American flag while speaking (Ad. Code 435-8), but you may have other flags as well.

D. Picketing. It has become traditional to picket in a moving circle, carrying signs. Policemen frequently believe that demonstrators *must* keep moving, but this is not the law (see speeches). A person who refuses to move on after being ordered by a policeman to do so may not be constitutionally arrested in the absence of some justification for the order. *Shuttlesworth v. City of Birmingham*, 382 U.S. 87 (1965). *No* permit is required to picket, and statutes provide for none. There is an informal rule that signs should not be on wooden sticks to prevent violence, but it is not a law.

E. Leafleting. All political leafleting on public streets is absolutely protected under the First Amendment. It is not littering or a violation of the Public Health Code, and Police Department regulations so recognize.

F. Sale of literature and buttons. When these activities are carried on as part of a demonstration and not for commercial purposes, they may not be penalized as peddling. *People v. Krebs*, 282 N.Y.S. 2d 996 (Crim. Ct. 1967); *People v. Hennacy*, 308 N.Y. 1039 (1955).

G. Use of tables, etc. Incidental use of tables to distribute political literature is protected under the First Amendment. It has been held not to violate the Administrative Code provisions penalizing obstructing the sidewalk (Ad. Code §692h-1.0). *People v. Katz*, 21 N.Y. 2d 132 (1967).

H. Sound equipment. To use sound equipment, you need a permit, and the provisions are probably constitutional (Ad. Code 435-6.0). A permit may not be denied arbitrarily.

II.
Demonstrations in Specialized Places

The rules described above for city streets are varied enormously in public places having restricted uses, and in private places. The charge used upon arrest is typically trespass rather than disorderly conduct. We will consider first certain types of public places.

A. Open thoroughfares in public buildings. The public has a right to demonstrate in public thoroughfares of specialized buildings, such as the Port Authority Terminal, *Wolin v. N.Y. Port*

3

Authority, 392 F.2d 83 (2nd Cir. 1968), and probably Lincoln Center Plaza. Specialized police may give you an argument, and should perhaps be consulted first.

B. Subways. The distribution of leaflets in the subway is protected, though subway regulations appear to forbid it on their face, *People v. St. Clair*, 288 N.Y.S. 2d 388 (Crim. Ct. 1968). Larger demonstrations may not be protected, because of the lack of space.

C. Parks. First Amendment rights in the parks are very similar to those in the street. Parks regulations seem on their face to require a permit for every activity including leafleting, but they are probably unconstitutional. *Rockwell v. Morris*, 211 N.Y.S. 2d 25 (I Dept. 1961) aff. 10 N.Y. 2d 721 (1961); *People v. Kaufman*, 264 N.Y.S. 2d 81 (Crim. Ct. 1965). It may be well to apply for such a permit. If you don't get it, you will then have a better defense if you are arrested.

D. Embassies. The police frequently argue that demonstrations near embassies are forbidden, and set up barricades accordingly. This is *not* the law, and demonstrations may be held near embassies. *People v. Solomonow, supra.*

E. Schools. Demonstrating around schools can be frustrating. Loitering in or near a school is a violation (P.L. 240.35[5]) and the statute has been held constitutionally applicable to distributing leaflets adjacent to a school. *People v. Sprowal*, 17 N.Y. 2d 884 (1966), app. dism. 385 U.S. 649. If the police tell you to move, ask them where to, and try to go there.

On the other hand, if you try to come as a guest to a school, as a speaker, for example, it is doubtful that the school can refuse to rent you its facilities or permit you to speak, *if it rents to others or permits others to speak. East Meadow Comm. Concerts Ass. v. Bd. of Ed.*, 18 N.Y. 2d 129 (1966). A public facility may not discriminate against certain speakers.

F. Private Places. In general, private landowners can exclude anyone they choose, for any reason. This rule is varied, however, in the light of three facts. (N.B. *These doctrines are not as well-settled as the foregoing and are to be viewed as entailing some risk of conviction.*)

1. **Private property open to the public.** In places which are used as public thoroughfares, it is likely that people have the same rights they have on publicly owned streets and may not rightfully be convicted of trespass. The outlying parking lot of a shopping center is a good example. *Amal. Food Employees Union, Local 590 v. Logan Valley Plaza, Inc.*, 88 S. Ct. 1601 (1968).

2. **Areas open to the public, necessary to reach the audience.** When a privately-owned place is open to the public, and demonstrators cannot reach their audience as effectively anywhere except on that place, the First Amendment *probably* protects the "trespasser." *Amal. Food Employees Union, Local, etc., supra.*

3. **Private enclaves.** Occasionally, you may want to reach the people in some enormous housing project. When such a development effectively encloses its residents, and insulates

4

them, and if it has areas ordinarily open to day to day traffic, you *probably* have a constitutional right to demonstrate in those areas. *Marsh v. Alabama*, 326 U.S. 501 (1945).

III.
Problems of Arrest

Certain aspects of the law of arrest may become relevant, especially the law of resisting arrest and interfering with an officer.

Any resistance, including passive resistance (e.g., sitting down) is resisting arrest. *People v. Crayton*, 284 N.Y.S. 2d 672 (I Dept. 1967).

A third party may be charged with interfering, for any physical interference, including *standing in the way*. Policemen frequently make such charges based on verbal interference (though the charges are probably not justified). *Keep quiet* and note badge number, car number, and any other facts. An arrested witness is almost no use at all, however justified he may be in the eyes of God.

Although the law may be subject to constitutional objections, resistance, *even to an unlawful arrest*, may be a crime. (The "no sock law," P.L. § 35.27).

Police Department
City of New York

February 25, 1969

TO ALL COMMANDS:

Subject: PROTECTION TO BE AFFORDED MEMBERS OF THE PRESS AND OTHER PERSONS RECORDING ACTIVITIES AT PUBLIC DEMONSTRATIONS

1. The attention of all members of the Department is called to the provisions of the Rules and Procedures, Chapter 2, paragraph 6.2, which states that "cooperation with the press, radio and television is vital to good relations."

2. Members of the Department should be aware that there are various groups and persons who are interested in gathering news and other information in relation to public activities besides members of the generally recognized news media, such as newspapers, or radio and television stations. There are news-gathering agencies and private citizens who do not necessarily possess press credentials from this Department but who have a valid interest in gathering news information. These people may represent small local newspapers, magazines, etc.

3. It has come to the attention of this Department that at public functions and demonstrations representatives of such news-gathering organizations and private citizens have experienced difficulty in the performance of their news-gathering function.

4. Members of this Department must be aware that even though members of such news-gathering organizations and private citizens may not possess official press credentials from this De-

partment, they have a right to gather the news as long as they do not violate the laws or other duly promulgated regulations. At the scenes of public functions or mass demonstrations, such persons are to be permitted to perform their functions provided that their actions do not interfere with Departmental operations or injure public safety.

5. Only members holding a working press card will be permitted within police and fire lines, in accordance with the provisions of the Rules and Procedures, Chapter 17, paragraph 148.2. However, other persons engaged in gathering news information should not be interfered with while working in otherwise non-restricted areas.

6. All persons engaged in news-gathering activities shall be expected to cooperate with this Department and obey all laws. If they do not, proper police action may be taken against them. If they are arrested and property is taken from them, such as notebooks, cameras, film, etc., such property is to be protected and dealt with in accordance with the Rules and Procedures.

7. One of the most precious freedoms that we enjoy in this country is that of freedom of the press, and no member of this Department shall do anything to interfere with the otherwise legitimate gathering of news be it by a reporter of a duly recognized news-gathering agency, a free-lance operator, or the representative of a small private publication.

8. Commanding officers and supervisory heads shall be responsible that members of their commands are instructed in and comply with the provisions of this order.

SANFORD D. GARELIK
Chief Inspector
T.O.P. 60

Police Department
City of New York

July 10, 1967

TO ALL COMMANDS:
Subject: LAWS CONCERNING THE DISTRIBUTION OF
HANDBILLS

1. At various times throughout the year, inquiries are received concerning the distribution of handbills, particularly with reference to those involving political and civil rights matters, and of the interpretation of the laws concerning same.

2. This area involves basic constitutional rights and the laws involved are Section 153.17 of the New York City Health Code and Section 755 (2)-7.0, subdivision 5 of the Administrative Code. Both sections of law are similar in language and intent and read as follows:

a. Section 153.17 of the Health Code entitled "Handbills and Circulars," reads as follows:

"No person shall throw, cast or distribute or permit to be thrown, cast or distributed, any handbills, circular, card, booklet, placard or other advertising matter in or upon any street, public place, frontyard, courtyard, stoop, vestibule, or hall of any building or letter box therein. *This section does not*

6

prohibit or otherwise regulate (1) the delivery of any matter by the United States postal service or (2) the distribution of sample copies of newspapers regularly sold by the copy or by annual subscription, *or (3) the distribution of anything other than commercial or business advertising matter.*" (Emphasis supplied.)

b. Section 755 (2)-7.0, subdivision 5 of the Administrative Code is essentially the same as Section 153.17 of the Health Code.

3. The courts have said a municipality may enact regulations in the interest of public safety, health, welfare or convenience, but these may not abridge the individual liberties secured by the Constitution to those who wish to speak, write, print or circulate information or opinion.

4. Members of the force must make a distinction for proper law enforcement between the distribution of handbills that contain commercial and business advertising and those circulars that relate to political objectives.

5. The above sections of law prohibit the distribution of advertising matter relating to commercial or business enterprises. However, circulars and handbills which deal with political matters, such as election of candidates, governmental operations, civil rights, foreign policy and any similar issues, may be freely and legally distributed on the streets of this City. Such distribution is an expression of opinion authorized by the Constitution.

BY DIRECTION OF THE POLICE COMMISSIONER.

SANFORD D. GARELIK
Chief Inspector
S.O.P. 12

Here are some of my thoughts on what legal observers should do at demonstrations:

1. Look like a lawyer. Dress like a lawyer, carry a yellow legal pad and, if you so desire, wear an armband which will identify you as a legal observer.

2. Do not stay in the crowd. Arrests will occur where the police are, and if you are in the crowd you will not be mobile and you will not be able to see very much. The best place to be, in order to see the most and be the most effective, is between the crowd and the police lines, or just behind the police. If the police chase you and you cannot win the argument that you should be able to stay there, then station yourself 20 or 30 feet behind the police lines or on the other side of the street. You should always be mobile so you can get to another part of the crowd quickly.

3. If an arrest and/or a police attack takes place, your job is to record as much of the facts as possible, for reconstruction

in court when necessary. The entire circumstances of the arrest are relevant. For example, you should note such factors as the size and general conduct of the crowd, locations of the people and police, the time, whether traffic was blocked, badge numbers of officers (particularly any who struck demonstrators and any who made arrests) and, very important, names and addresses of witnesses.

4. Unless you fear beatings of arrestees, which in New York usually happens only when the arrestees are pretty far left or gay, or the demonstration was violent or the police were called pigs, it is not advisable to follow arrestees to the police station. They will probably not be questioned about the arrest so your presence is not necessary to prevent incriminating statements, and you can be more useful remaining at the demonstration. Ideally, another lawyer should be at the police station.

5. If you have been working with the group or groups that are demonstrating, and if they so desire, you can introduce yourself to the commanding officer and tell him you are there to act as a legal observer. Whenever applicable, you can inform him that the demonstrators do not wish to be arrested and that you are there to act as a liaison between the demonstrators and the police. At peaceful demonstrations the police will usually be reluctantly cooperative. They have few definite guidelines for such situations and if you act as though you know what you are doing the results can be surprising. For example, where squatters and their supporters are illegally in an apartment, your statement to the police that the owner must be personally present to tell them to leave may prevent an arrest. If the superintendent is there, you can ask him, in the presence of the police, whether the owner authorized him to tell the squatters to leave; to point out the super's lack of authority, ask him if he has the authority to select tenants for vacant apartments, sign leases, etc. Likewise, where the police are improperly ordering demonstrators to disperse you can try talking the commanding officer out of dispersing or arresting the crowd by citing some law and telling him that he can't do what he's doing. It sometimes works.

6. In non-violent demonstrations of this type your function can also be to make the arrest as smooth and peaceful as

possible and, by advising the demonstrators exactly when they are going to be arrested and that they should not resist, avoiding charges of resisting arrest. Resisting arrest is a misdemeanor and when the only other charge is disorderly conduct (a violation, which is less than a crime), avoiding the misdemeanor charge makes the arrest relatively insignificant.

B. Violent Demonstrations

At violent demonstrations the presence of a lawyer is even more important. Windows may be broken, rocks and bottles may be thrown, and the reason for the demonstration is usually pretty far left. Also, at any leftist demonstration the police may attack the demonstrators, unfounded arrests are not uncommon, and the charges will be much more serious, usually including a few felonies.

Although bottles and rocks are usually thrown from the rear of the crowd or from rooftops, people are often grabbed from the front edges or body of the crowd and charged with throwing things. Often the apparent leaders or the most vocal demonstrators are the ones arrested. Also, the police often arbitrarily assign the carrying of missiles or weapons and the breaking of windows to those arrested. The more violent or further left the demonstration, the more likely the police are to attack, chase and beat people, whom they then arrest. These attacks are usually at a particular area of the crowd; those attacked are in the wrong place at the wrong time and if they are beaten by the police they will almost invariably be charged with assault or resisting arrest, and possibly riot or inciting to riot. For example, at the arrest of demonstrators protesting the war, racism and the country's policies in general, near the Waldorf-Astoria where Nixon was attending a banquet, a Vietcong flag was hoisted on a flagpole in front of a nearby building. The police commanding officer is quoted in *The New York Times* as saying, "I saw red," and the *Times* article reports that the police formed a wedge, attacked the crowd between themselves and the flagpole, arrested several people, and took the flag down.

The task of legal observers at violent demonstrations is much more difficult than at peaceful demonstrations. In addition to noting all the things described in the previous section, observers

9

must constantly watch for the direction bottles and rocks are coming from, which arrestees, if any, were carrying weapons or missiles, how and by whom windows were broken, the relationship in time and space of broken windows to arrests, police provocations, badge numbers of actual arresting officers, whether any police officers are injured and if so their injuries and badge numbers, and what injuries arrestees appear to have as they are being led off to the paddy wagon. Observations of injuries are important because officers claim injuries that they did not sustain, and because demonstrators who are beaten either en route to or in the police station are said by the police to have suffered their injuries at the time of arrest, while assaulting a policeman or resisting arrest. Of particular importance are names and addresses of witnesses. Photographs, movies, times, places, relative times and locations, and all other surrounding circumstances are also obviously important. The events at demonstrations happen quickly and tumultuously and no observer will be able to gather more than part of all the data needed. After everyone has gotten out of jail, a meeting of all witnesses and arrestees should be held so that the facts can be organized and pieced together.

A must reading for lawyers who wish to act as observers and advisers at demonstrations is *The Bust Book*, published by Grove Press and available in paperback bookstores.

C. Non-Demonstration Arrests

Obviously, a lawyer will have few occasions to observe non-demonstration arrests and where a lawyer does see an arrest, it will usually be a situation where he or she does not know the arrestee and the lawyer is there by chance.

From the observer's point of view these arrests fall into two types: (1) where the crime is committed on the spot, such as disorderly conduct, possession of drugs, or perhaps burglary or robbery, and (2) where the crime was committed at some earlier time and the arrestee is being taken into custody as a suspect. In the latter category, which includes generally more serious crimes such as burglary, robbery or drug sales to undercover agents, there is little a lawyer can do other than overhear conversations to detect admissions being made without *Miranda* warnings (see Chapter 7).

Where the crime is committed in the officer's and lawyer's presence the lawyer can be valuable simply as a witness to the crime and as to whether there was any police misconduct. For example, a lawyer's quiet observation of an illegal search and of the place where contraband was found, can be crucial in discrediting the common "dropsey" story told by police officers at hearings on motions to suppress evidence on the ground that it is the result of an illegal search. (The "dropsey" story, heard several times a day in various parts of the courthouse, goes roughly as follows: "As I approached the defendant, the defendant dropped something to the ground. Without losing sight thereof, I picked it up, examined it, found it to be apparent contraband, and placed the defendant under arrest.") Similarly, observations of searches of automobiles and occupants can refute police officers' stories that they saw the contraband in open view while routinely requesting identification of the car and driver.

For other arrests, such as arrests for disorderly conduct, harassment, interfering with governmental administration, resisting arrest, etc., the precise actions of the parties, conversations, and the surrounding circumstances should be noted. Witnesses' names and addresses should also be taken down.

If you see an illegal search or other police misconduct, my own opinion is that the best thing to do is stand back and watch, unless the officer is beating the arrestee in which case your interference might stop the beating. Afterward you can find out the name of the arrestee from the log book of the police station and his address from the court papers and you can then get in touch with the defendant or simply come to court the next time the case is on the calendar. If you interfere at the time of arrest you may be arrested yourself and you will also alert the officer to your presence so that, if he was planning to use the dropsey story, he might change his story.

For the more serious crimes committed in the presence of the police officer, a lawyer can be a witness just like any other citizen. If the person arrested did not really commit the crime and the lawyer is a witness, he can of course testify to that fact.

11

If the defendant is caught in the act, such as running down the street with a pocketbook, followed by a screaming woman, there is really nothing anyone can do.

For the more serious arrests, especially where the arrest follows the commission of the crime by some period of time, statements by the defendant become significant. The important and often disputed facts are whether the statement was made at all, the time and place the statement was made, and whether the *Miranda* warnings were given prior to questioning. For example, the police grab an average looking teen-age boy who fits a description of a robber, search him in a hallway and find a large amount of money on him. Their question: "where did you get this" would lead to inadmissible admissions if the *Miranda* warnings were not given, because if he was searched he had to be under arrest or effectively detained. In this case the police may later testify that admissions were made at the police station, after *Miranda* warnings were given, and a witness' observation of the arrest can change the entire case. Remember that what appears to be an exculpatory statement can in fact be a damaging admission if it is later proven to be untrue or if the defendant changes his story. Note that the search in this case might also be illegal and so an onlooker's observations can be very important; see Chapter 7.

If you wish to advise someone who is being arrested or questioned that he should make no statements at all, you better do so in the first phrase you speak to the arrestee; the first words to you from the officer following your remarks will probably be unprintable and any further advice from you to the arrestee may lead to your arrest on a charge of interfering with governmental administration.

Chapter 2

THE POLICE STATION

Lawyers often ask whether they should go to the police station in response to a call from an arrestee. The question really is: is there anything that a lawyer can do at the precinct house? The answer, as with everything, depends on the case.

The most important act a lawyer can perform at the police station is to prevent the arrestee from making incriminating statements. Where there is a possibility of self-incrimination it is important for the lawyer to get to the police station immediately. If the arrestee knows what he is doing, he will ask that he be permitted to call his lawyer. Usually the officer will comply, sometimes only after a delay, but you may not be able to speak to your client directly. If you are permitted to speak to him, the best advice is for him to say nothing until you arrive. If you cannot speak to him, get the officer's name, note the time of your call, and tell the officer that you represent the arrestee and that you do not wish him to be questioned until you arrive; also ask that the officer give your client the message, while you hang on so that you can hear it, that he should make no statements at all until you arrive.

Self-incriminating statements are a problem only in certain types of cases; common sense will tell which cases present this problem. Generally there will be no questioning at all in demonstration cases, street crimes such as disorderly conduct or fighting, drug busts where the officer claims to have seen the arrestee in possession, and generally any other crime that the officer claims to have seen take place. Conversely, there will usually be questioning in cases such as homicide, robbery, burglary, forgery, etc., where the officer did not see the crime and where the arrestee is being accused by another citizen or by some other evidence. The questioning usually takes place immediately following the arrest, although in very serious cases an Assistant District Attorney may be called and the questioning may continue for hours.

If you can reach your client before he talks, the best advice is for him to say nothing at that time. Even if his statements can be exculpatory, they are best made later after being thought about so that they can be presented in the best possible manner. It may also be advantageous, depending on the circumstances, to make the statements directly to an Assistant District Attorney, in return for some other consideration, or to submit the defendant to a private lie detector test before the statements are made. The defendant's mere denial of the crime, or claim of an alibi, are meaningless; the arrest has been made and cannot be reversed. Denials and claims of alibis are matters of defense and, if made in the police station, will not serve to free the defendant but may be used to impeach a later, different story.

The question of whether a statement is self-incriminating is a complicated one and should be broadly interpreted by lawyers. If an arrest takes place in an apartment and is based on drugs having been found in the apartment, then giving that apartment as his home address can be self-incriminating. Law professors have argued that there are circumstances under which revealing one's name can be incriminating, such as where a bookmaker who is known only by name is arrested, or where contraband is found in a package with a name on it. You can inform your client that he is not under oath in the police station. Refusal to give a name or giving a name that the officer knows is false, however, will result in the defendant being booked as John Doe and held without bail. Likewise, refusal to submit to fingerprinting where the offense is a printable one, which now includes all misdemeanors and felonies, will also result in being held without bail. Conversely, where the police are trying to harass your client by printing him on a non-printable offense, you should instruct your client not to submit to fingerprinting, and the police will then not attempt to get prints since it is impossible to print someone against his will. Incidentally, many police precincts have a list on the wall of offenses which are printable.

There are many other functions for a lawyer at the police precinct aside from avoiding self-incrimination. The police always inquire into the prior criminal record of the arrestee. If the arrestee will be fingerprinted, the yellow sheet (the record of priors) that appears at the arraignment will generally contain only prior fingerprinted cases in this jurisdiction. Another more complete yellow sheet from national files is mailed to the officer a few weeks later. If the arrestee will not be finger-printed, the officer will telephone the Bureau of Criminal Information (called BCI) and he will be told over the phone the prior record of the person with the arrestee's name and birthdate. BCI records only contain priors in which the defendant was fingerprinted at some point in the case.

Section 160.10 of the Criminal Procedure Law provides that the police must fingerprint persons arrested for any misde-meanor or felony, and for loitering for purposes of committing prostitution. Only arrests for offenses classified as violations (not crimes) such as disorderly conduct, harassment, loitering for other than prostitution or drugs, and criminal trespass in the fourth degree are now not printable after arrest. Copies of prints are sent to both Albany and Washington. Upon conviction, prints are taken again to record the result of the case, except that the District Attorney can waive fingerprints following a conviction of a violation. In practice D.A.'s waive prints only where there is a guilty plea; if there is a conviction of a violation after trial a waiver of prints is very difficult to get, although it should perhaps be sought. A waiver of prints is very important and should be sought as a condition of the plea to a violation, since if there are no prints taken there is no easily findable record of the case. This is especially important for politically active people who are likely to be rearrested. If a case is eventu-ally dismissed, § 79e of the Civil Rights Law says that the police must return the prints, provided that the defendant has not pre-viously been convicted of a crime or of disorderly conduct. There is of course no way to get the copy back from the federal government but getting prints back is still important, especially for first offenders, so that if they are arrested again their yellow sheet, which is initially prepared from state records, will be clean. This can have an enormous effect on a later case, on bail, plea bargaining, and sentencing. The procedure for getting prints back is to get a transcript (fee $1) from the general clerk's office (Room 450 in New York County) and bring it to the

Bureau of Criminal Information, 400 Broome Street, New York, N. Y.

Arrestees accused of any misdemeanor or violation are eligible for release from the police station upon the issuance of an appearance ticket (formerly known as a Vera summons). An appearance ticket is somewhat like a traffic ticket; it simply directs the defendant to appear in court for arraignment at some later date. Its issuance can also be conditioned on the posting of bail at the police precinct, in amounts up to $500 for Class A misdemeanors, $250 for Class B's, and $100 for violations. The issuance of an appearance ticket and the amount of bail, if any, is discretionary with the police. The desk officer may refuse to issue a ticket if he has reason to believe it could lead to a continuation of disorders. If the desk officer is refusing to issue a summons simply because he is angry at the defendant, a complaint to his superior or even to the Civilian Complaint Review Board, 200 Park Avenue South, New York, N.Y., 673-6001 (day or night), can reverse his decision.

The procedure for release on a ticket is that the officer fills out a several-page questionnaire on the defendant's background with the defendant getting varying numbers of points depending on his answers. The most points are gotten by having the greatest roots in the community. The defendant must also furnish a reference who verifies his identity and address, either by telephone or in person. If the defendant gets more than a certain number of points he is released on a summons and arraigned at some later date. A lawyer can be helpful in this process by, for example, getting a reference who has no telephone down to the police station, or even acting as a reference himself if he knows the defendant.

In some cases, particularly political ones (in the broad sense), defendants may be beaten unless a lawyer stays with them. A lawyer's presence is also much appreciated by his client simply for providing moral support, food (a man arrested in the afternoon will probably not be fed until the next morning), cigarettes (should be non-filter), and simply contact with the outside world. Lawyers should contact family and friends about appearing in court and posting bail, and the bail facts, described in Chapter 3, can be gotten from the defendant at the police station.

The first thing that happens when the police officer and the defendant arrive at the police station is that the police officer interviews the complaining witness, if any, and prepares a report on the alleged crime. The officer must also fill out reports on the arrest and the defendant is asked his name, address, prior criminal record, employment or occupation, etc. Questioning about the crime may also begin at this time. If the offense is printable the prints are taken in the local precinct. If the arrestee is to be photographed, he is transported to one of several places throughout the city where such photographs are taken. Transportation of prisoners following arrest is usually not done by an ordinary patrol car; the officer has to call the transportation division of the Department of Correction and there is usually some delay. The prisoner is then taken to court and turned over to the Department of Correction, which puts him in a special detention pen where he will await arraignment (in New York this pen is on the third floor of the courthouse). Shortly before his case is called the prisoner is placed in a small pen directly behind the bench of the arraignment part and sometimes you can talk to him there, although often only Legal Aid attorneys are permitted in that room.

Chapter 3

THE ARRAIGNMENT

The arraignment is the first court proceeding for all persons arrested. Its purpose is to inform the defendant of the charges against him, to set bail, and then to adjourn the case to a hearing or trial part. The New York County Criminal Court averages over 250 arraignments per day so each one is a very quick proceeding. In New York County arraignments take place in Part AR1 on the first floor of the Criminal Courts building at 100 Centre Street.

There are legal requirements that arraignments take place within a certain amount of time after the arrest, but, since those requirements are virtually always met in New York, they will not be discussed here. If a person is arrested in the morning, he will usually be arraigned in the afternoon or, if the court is crowded, in the evening. A person arrested in the afternoon will usually be arraigned in the evening while a person arrested in the evening or late at night will be arraigned sometime the next day. The day session begins at about 10:00 A.M. and ends at exactly 5:00 P.M. while night court begins approximately 8:15 P.M. and ends around 1:00 A.M.

Preparing for an arraignment should begin with preparing yourself for a long stay, perhaps by bringing a book. The arresting officer has the complaint prepared in the complaint room (room 450 in New York County) and the lawyer can wait for the officer to bring the complaint to the arraignment part in the clerk's office of Part AR1. It is first come, first served for arresting officers in getting complaints drawn and you may have to wait for hours. The only way to get some idea about when the complaint will come down is to find the arresting officer in the complaint room and ask him when he thinks his turn will come. When the complaint comes, fill out a Notice of Appearance, give it to the clerk, get a copy of the complaint from him, and copy the yellow sheet if there is one. If you have not yet had a chance to talk to your client to get the bail facts from him, ask the police officer to go into the pens and bring your client out. Usually only Legal Aid Society lawyers are permitted in the pens. In New York County there are benches near the pens where attorneys and clients can confer. If the case is called before you have finished talking, tell the court that you are not ready and ask for a second call, which will be granted.

When your case is reached the court officer will call the defendant's name and you and he will step up to the table in front of the bench, with him on your left. The clerk will ask you to note your appearance which simply means that you tell the court stenographer your name and address and whom you represent if there is more than one defendant. The clerk will then quickly ask you if you waive the reading of the rights and charges, to which you should answer that you do. If you do not waive the reading of the rights and charges everything in the courtroom will stop, the clerk will give you a puzzled look, everyone will immediately know that you are a novice, and the clerk will then unintelligibly read the complaint and recite a little speech about the fact that the defendant has a right to a lawyer, an adjournment to get a lawyer, and a trial before a one- or three-man bench, etc. After "waiving the reading," as it is called for short, you then make your brief speech.

The lawyer's plea should be brief but forcefully presented (the courtroom is very noisy) and should contain the bail facts in their most favorable light together with any other facts that can persuade the judge to parole (release without bail) the defendant or set as low a bail as possible. A sampling of the data that is commonly called "bail facts" are the following: the number of years the defendant has lived in New York City or the Metropolitan area, the defendant's job record and earnings, the amount of time he has lived at one address, whether the defendant lives with his parents, whether the defendant has a family and whether he supports his family, his educational background, the people who are now in court to appear for him (who should be told beforehand to stand behind the railing when the case is called), and any other facts that indicate

19

stability and ties to the community, such as civic work. Priors and the nature of the case are also important, as described below.

Where applicable, it may be helpful to make a motion to dismiss on the law. For example, where many people are arrested in an apartment and charged with violating § 240.36 of the Penal Law, loitering for the purpose of using drugs, you can move to dismiss on the ground that it is impossible to loiter in an apartment since loitering is hanging about without an apparent purpose and one does not need a purpose in being in an apartment. Such motions by the defense lawyer almost never succeed but the judge may become convinced that the case is weak and he may therefore agree to parole or a low bail.

The defendant's prior record is very important; the longer the record, the higher the bail. If the yellow sheet (the sheet showing the defendant's prior record, which is obtained only if the defendant is fingerprinted) shows no prior record, you can say "he has a clean yellow sheet." Perhaps you can ask the arresting officer if he knows of prior arrests that are not included on the yellow sheet. The yellow sheets often indicate only the date of arrest and the charges without indicating the final outcome of the case. The defendant should be asked what the outcome of those cases was, and if all prior arrests were later dismissed, you can correctly point out to the court that the defendant has no prior convictions. If necessary, you can check the outcome of the priors yourself in the record room (room 450 in New York County). Docket numbers can be found only under the date of arrest, so you will have to copy the dates of arrest from the yellow sheet. If any of the priors are of an unusual nature, such as a statutory rape charge which is later dismissed because the defendant married the complainant, that should be pointed out to the court. Likewise, if a prior drug arrest was for marijuana, the court should be so informed. Where the defendant has a long yellow sheet it can either not be mentioned, or, if you have the energy, you can pull out the records of his prior cases and if it's true, point out to the court that the defendant has proven his reliability in appearing whenever required in all his prior cases. Since the purpose of bail is to insure the defendant's presence in court, this defendant should be paroled since he has proven his reliability. Of course, the reality is that where a person has a long record the purpose of bail is not to insure his presence in court but to insure that he remains in jail, and arguments along these lines will probably be ineffectual. The courts have actually been practicing preventive detention all along by setting bails that the courts know cannot be made.

The following are some of my thoughts about particular types of cases. In occasional political cases, such as a mini-riot where only a few arrests are made, it may be wiser as far as bail is concerned to minimize the court's awareness of the political nature of the case. This can be done simply by quickly presenting the bail facts and doing nothing else, which takes advantage of the extreme time pressures on the court. Conversely, in other cases before relatively progressive judges (of which there are few), it may be helpful to briefly discuss the politics of the arrest. It depends on the case and the judge.

A related question is whether, when the defendant has been beaten, the lawyer should make a stink about this and specifically state for the record that the defendant has been beaten. My own opinion is that doing so is contra-productive in most cases. The fact that the minutes of the arraignment will show that the lawyer informed the court that the defendant was beaten is irrelevant and not even admissible in later proceedings. Furthermore, with some judges it will result in higher, not lower, bail since the judge assumes that if the defendant was beaten, he belongs in jail. A much better practice is for the lawyer to make careful notes of his observations of the defendant's injuries and, if the defendant gets out on bail, arrange for pictures to be taken of the injuries as soon as possible. Remember that the person who takes the pictures may have to testify in order for them to be admissible. He should also be taken to a hospital or doctor to further document the injuries. Where the defendant will not be able to get out on bail, you should ask that the court order that medical treatment be given, and the court will so endorse the papers. If he is treated there will be a record of his injuries in a doctor's handwriting, signed by the doctor.

Where a great many people are arrested the court will try to rush the proceedings along. The judge may try to cut short your statements and limit the time you have to talk to the arrestees, but, in order to adequately represent your clients you need time to confer, prepare your statements and speak. Where the charges are light, a conference with the judge in his chambers or at the bench, in which you hint that there may be long delays since there is a shortage of lawyers to interview and represent the arrestees, may produce a blanket agreement of parole, or perhaps parole for all persons in certain categories.

Where there is a mass arrest with only one or a few complaining witnesses, as in a sit-in at a welfare center where the complainant is a welfare official, identification may become one of the principal issues of the case. To avoid the complainant having an additional opportunity to identify the defendants, it may be advantageous for you to advise your clients not to stand when their names are called and for you to formally move that the complainant be excluded from the courtroom during the arraignment in order not to taint any later identifications. The Lawyers Guild, 1 Hudson Street, New York, N. Y., has a memo on this subject. Whether the court will grant the motion is hard to predict since such motions have been made on very few occasions and the results have been varied.

If your clients are mothers on welfare, have the children stand behind the rail and inform the court that there is no one else to care for the kids. In some cases it may be helpful to point out the reason for the demonstration, such as where it was for food or clothing.

Another technique is to stress the favorable points to such an extent that the court overlooks the fact that you have not mentioned certain important factors. For example, in a recent case three defendants were charged with disorderly conduct when they blocked an intersection in a protest against the fact that there was no school crossing guard at the intersection. The lawyer began by making a short speech about the reason for the demonstration, that it was non-violent, that the reason for the demonstration itself showed that the defendants had roots in the community, that one defendant was a school teacher, had never been arrested before, had lived all her life in New York City, had lived five years in one apartment, etc., same kind of facts about the second defendant, and by the time the lawyer began discussing the third defendant the judge had already granted parole to all three. In fact, the third defendant had a heavy criminal record and had spent time in jail for a militant political act. It is true that in a more serious case the judge would probably have remembered to ask about priors but he may have reached a decision before learning about the defendant's priors and, in a proceeding as fast as an arraignment, a judge's first impulse is most important.

When your client is on parole or probation and the charges are light, or in any case that doesn't appear to have a chance of being won, you should consider pleading him at the arraignment to a violation and, in return for the early plea, getting a waiver of fingerprints. Of course, this can only be done where the defendant was not fingerprinted before coming to court. In practice, a plea to a violation with a waiver of fingerprints will not be reported to the Bureau of Criminal Information and the parole or probation officer will not be officially informed of the arrest. In effect, there is no findable record of the occurrence.

Occasionally persons under 16 years of age exaggerate their age and wind up in the criminal court. If the age of under 16 can be documented, by a birth certificate or by the testimony of the mother, the criminal court must and will dismiss the action for lack of jurisdiction. The arresting officer will then immediately take the defendant to Family Court where he will be reprocessed from the beginning.

For males over 17 years of age where the charges are not too heavy and non-political in nature, and the defendant is not employed and does not have too long a record, consider trying to enroll him in the Manhattan Court Employment Project, commonly known as the Vera project. Representatives from the Vera project are in the courtroom or in the clerk's office and can be spotted by looking for the young, bright, hipper-looking men and women with clipboards. This program will be more fully discussed in Chapter 5.

Where the defendants are in arraignment court in response to a summons issued to them at the police station, the arraignment is a mere formality and your presence is not necessary. Since they have already shown that their ties to the community are sufficient to permit the issuance of a summons, and since they are already proving their reliability by appearing in response to the summons, the D.A. almost invariably consents to parole, without any speeches on the defendant's ties to the community, and the matter is adjourned.

The waiting period for an arraignment can be very long (up to 6 or 7 hours), and, even in certain non-summons cases, a lawyer might properly feel that his absence from the arraignment will not make any difference and his time can be better spent elsewhere. This is true where, for example, the judge who is sitting is lenient, the charge is very minor, and the defendant has roots in the community and no prior record; parole is virtually certain in such cases. The lawyer's absence does not mean that the defendant is unrepresented since the Legal Aid Society will handle any case in which the defense lawyer is not actually in the courtroom at the time of the arraignment. However, in heavy cases or where the bail facts are not favorable, a non-Legal Aid lawyer's presence can make a difference. Also where the arrestees are Movement people, the lawyer should always appear at the arraignment both to show the people that they are supported by their lawyers and to allay their fears.

After bail is set, the matter is adjourned to a date convenient to the police officer and the defense counsel. Where there is some doubt about whether the defendant will make bail, the adjournment must, of course, be a short one, not longer than a week or ten days.

Under the old code a complaint based entirely on hearsay (e.g., in alleged sales to undercover agents the arresting officer, not the undercover agent, would swear out the complaint) was called a short affidavit. Section 55 of the Criminal Court Act limited adjournments to no longer than 2 days where a defendant was being held on a short, but this rule was universally ignored either by adjourning it for longer periods of time or by the court granting several adjournments until there was an indictment. The new law changes this substantially in several ways. First of all there are now several different kinds of accusatory instruments, enumerated and defined in § 100.10 of the C.P.L. The three most important are misdemeanor complaints, felony complaints, and informations (for misdemeanors). The important points to note are that complaints, both misdemeanor and felony, need state only a probable cause to arrest and can be based on hearsay. Complaints can now be sworn out either in the police station or in court. If it is done in the precinct this means that the complainant need not be present in court for the arraignment, a definite disadvantage to a defense counsel who wants to talk to the complainant. Informations however must state a prima facie case and must consist of testamentary evidence, not hearsay. A misdemeanor complaint can be accompanied by supporting affidavits, and if the combination of the complaint and affidavits eliminates all hearsay, they can be held to be equivalent to an information. All of the above will contain a brief narrative of the facts, unlike the accusatory instruments which are prepared after the matter is submitted to the grand jury. If the grand jury charges the defendant with a misdemeanor then a prosecutor's information is filed; if a felony then an indictment is filed.

A defendant cannot be tried on a misdemeanor complaint; unless he waives prosecution by information, an information must be prepared. Whether to waive depends on the case; often no additional useful information can be gotten from an information and waiving will not hurt. The defendant must demand that an information be prepared. If he is in jail, and he makes such a demand (orally, in court), and an information is not filed within 5 days, excluding Sundays, then the defendant must be released on his own recognizance, unless the state can show good cause for the delay (§170.70). Be prepared to argue that the D.A.'s reasons are not good cause, especially since release does not mean dismissal of the case.

In felony cases a complaint, including hearsay, is sufficient to hold the defendant until indictment. However, §180.80 of the C.P.L. directs that an accused in custody be released if there is no preliminary hearing within 72 hours of arrest, unless, of course, the state shows good cause why the accused should not be released, or an indictment has come down, or the defendant requested a further adjournment. If the past is any indication, most judges will accept almost any excuse for not releasing the defendant, and they will continue to deny preliminary hearings in homicide and drug-sale cases. Your only arguments are that good cause is not being shown, and that release does not mean dismissal of the charges. You can of course challenge the continued detention by writ of habeas corpus.

Chapter 4

THE PARTS OF THE COURT AND THE ROUTE
A CASE FOLLOWS; FELONIES; INTERVIEWING YOUR
CLIENT; BENCH WARRANTS; BAIL APPLICATIONS

A. The Parts of The Court and The Route A Case Follows

The parts of the court changed in name, function, and, to some extent, efficiency in Spring, 1971. The route that a case follows is shown in the diagram on the next page. It will be helpful to refer to the diagram when reading the following paragraphs.

A portion of the adult (over 19) misdemeanor cases, and some felony cases to go the Master All Purpose (MAP) Part. This is an experimental part designed to increase the efficiency of the court and it has several features that other parts do not have. Cases can be postponed by telephone (566-7381 in Manhattan) or letter, pursuant to certain guidelines. Valid grounds for adjournment are illness, actual engagement in another court, being out of town, and extraordinary emergencies. The court must be notified at least 48 hours prior to the scheduled court appearance, except for emergencies arising later, and the guidelines provide that only two adjournments will be permitted in any case. It should be noted that the only major advantage of these guidelines is that the adjournments can be accomplished by phone or letter, which spares the defendant and complainant from having to go to court. However, it has always been possible to adjourn a case in any part (provided the case is not too old and there have not been more than one or two adjournments at the defendant's request) simply by giving the defendant an affidavit to take to court. Acceptable grounds have always included actual engagement or being out of town, and where there are real emergencies a telephone call or telegram has always sufficed. All of this is still true for the other parts.

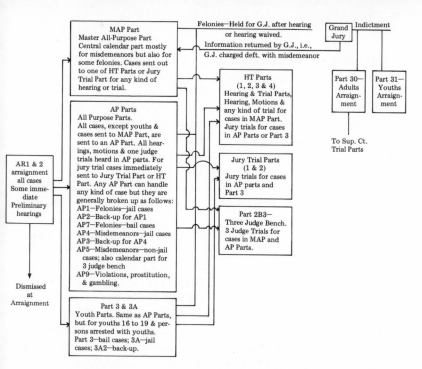

The MAP Part also has a sign-in procedure in the hallway outside the courtroom, so that the case is not called until everyone is present. There are extra Assistant District Attorneys assigned to the part so that there can be a conference between defense lawyer and A.D.A. before the case is called, instead of while the case is before the bench as it is now done. This is one of the times when plea bargaining takes place (see Chapter 10). So far there has generally been a lenient judge assigned to the MAP Part so if a plea is indicated in the case, it would not be unwise to plead right away in the MAP Part.

The MAP Part is a calendar part and it is very crowded. If, after a conference with a D.A., it is decided that both sides are ready for a hearing, motion, or trial, the case is called and sent out to one of the four Hearing and Trial (HT) Parts. These parts handle any kind of proceeding before a single judge, and they also handle jury trials. Assignments are made on the basis of which part is free when the case is sent out. If the proceeding is something other than a trial, and the case continues, it is usually sent back to the MAP Part, but sometimes it is adjourned to the HT Part for trial.

27

All non-youth cases not sent to the MAP Part are sent to one of the All Purpose (AP) Parts. Although each part can handle any kind of case, particular kinds of cases are generally sent to specific parts. If, however, a case changes while it is in an AP Part, such as a felony being reduced to a misdemeanor, it will remain in that part. Jail felony cases usually go to AP1; bailed felony cases to AP7; jailed and bailed misdemeanors go to AP3 or AP5; violations, prostitution and gambling cases go to AP9. Violations are always handled from start to finish in AP9, or a back-up part for it, since there are no proceedings in violation cases other than trial before one judge. Prostitution cases leave AP9 only when a three-judge bench is requested, which is rare.

The above mentioned AP Parts are "calendar" parts; other AP Parts are "back-up" parts for the calendar parts. All the cases that are "on the calendar" for that day are listed on a mimeographed list which is posted outside the courtroom. The length of the calendar varies enormously, from 30 to 120 or more cases. Cases are called in the calendar part each morning beginning shortly after 9:30. Attorneys can get their cases called early simply by giving the calendar number to the "bridge man," who calls the cases, or the "rail man," who stands at the rail which separates the bench area from the seating area. When the case is called, all parties, including complainants and police officers, go before the court and if both sides are ready for a hearing, motion, or trial, the case is marked "ready" and sent to a back-up part for the proceeding. When the calendar part has completed the call of the calendar, which occurs in late morning or sometime in the afternoon depending on how long the calendar is on that day, then it too becomes a hearing part. Occasionally there is no back-up part, due to a shortage of judges for that day, and all cases must wait for the calendar part to complete its business. Ordinarily AP2 is the back-up part for AP1 and AP7, AP4 is the back-up part for AP3, 3A2 is the back-up part for Part 3, and occasionally other back-up parts are added where needed. Parts HT1, 2, 3 and 4 are the back-ups for the Master All Purpose Part. In some cases, except in the MAP Part, where the calendar is not too heavy you can increase the chances of having the hearing or motion before the calendar judge by not requesting that the case be called early. Likewise, you can assure that the case will be heard by the back-up judge if it is called early in the day.

Where one or more of the defendants is between the ages of 16 and 19 the case is sent to the Youth Part, where Part 3 is for persons out of jail and Part 3A is for persons in jail. The Part 3 complex handles all aspects of misdemeanor cases where one or more defendants is a youth, from preliminary hearing through motions and trial, unless a three-man bench or jury trial is requested in which case the matter is transferred to a jury part (Jury Part I or II, or HT1, 2, 3 or 4) or Part 2B3. Felony cases where one or more of the defendants is a youth are also sent to Part 3 where, as in adult cases, the Criminal Court has jurisdiction only until indictment, and only for purposes of setting bail, holding a preliminary hearing, or reducing the case to a misdemeanor.

In Class A (maximum one year) misdemeanor cases where the defendant is an adult or a youth not granted Youthful Offender treatment, the defendant has a choice of trial by one judge, three judges, or six-man jury. Choice of the manner of trial is made after the preliminary hearing (or waiver thereof) and after the hearing on motions is completed. At this time a not guilty plea is also entered, which is of course revocable at any time that the defendant desires to plead guilty. As between the three choices, most experienced and aggressive lawyers prefer a jury, as discussed in more detail in Chapter 11B. As to the choice between one- and three-judge benches, my own opinion is that it is generally advantageous to choose the three-judge panel but the decision also depends on who is sitting on the three-judge bench and who will be the one-judge trier of fact. Three-judge trials are desirable because the trials are more formal and move slower, and there are three judges who ask questions and confer when deciding motions, which gives you more time to think. Part 2B3 handles the three-judge trials and, although in the past they have sometimes not been able to reach all the cases sent to them, since the advent of jury trials they have been able to handle all their cases.

Persons accused of Class B misdemeanors (maximum 3 months) are not entitled to a jury trial in New York City, although they can elect to be tried by a jury outside New York City. The reasons for this are historical and have no reasonable basis today. If you desire a jury in a Class B case in New York

29

City you should request it and argue that it is a denial of equal protection to be able to have a jury only if you live outside New York City. Your request will almost certainly be denied, however, and your only remedy is an appeal after conviction.

The right to a jury trial of youths between 16 and 19 is complicated under the new law and is discussed in detail in Chapter 8.

B. Felonies

The Criminal Court, as mentioned above, has jurisdiction over felonies only for setting bail and holding preliminary hearings, and only until such time as an indictment is handed down by the grand jury. As soon as an indictment is filed the Criminal Court loses jurisdiction of the case entirely, and it has been held that the defendant has lost his right to a preliminary hearing. The only other thing that can happen to felonies in the Criminal Court is that they can be reduced to misdemeanors either on motion of the Assistant District Attorney or on rare occasion by the judge after a preliminary hearing.

Many cases in which the facts technically constitute a felony begin as a felony complaint, but are later reduced on motion of an A.D.A. in Criminal Court to a misdemeanor. The reasons for this are to reduce the caseload of the Supreme Court, where trials are long, and also because the D.A. feels that a misdemeanor sentence would be sufficient, based on the nature of the crime and the defendant's past record. Reductions are especially common in youth cases, since youths without records rarely go to jail and the court could in a heavier case sentence a youth, even one who has been granted Youthful Offender treatment (see Chapter 8), to 3 months or a year, depending on whether the underlying charge is a B or A misdemeanor, respectively. Another reason for reductions to misdemeanors is that many cases, although technically felonies, will not lead to an indictment if submitted to the grand jury, especially if the defendant is young or the crime is relatively minor.

Examples of cases frequently reduced on motion of the D.A. are minor assaults on police officers, auto theft where the crime was apparently committed for the purpose of joy-riding rather than re-selling the car, drug cases of relatively low quantities, criminal possession of stolen property, larcenies not too much over the dividing line of $250.00, and, occasionally, burglaries and purse snatchings without any violence to the victim. Demonstration cases, where the felony charges are riot and assault on police officers, are usually reduced to misdemeanors but this depends on the nature of the demonstration, the overall political climate, the D.A. in charge of these cases, who the defendants are, and the lawyer's skill in negotiating. Cases almost never reduced are robberies, burglaries where the government suspects that the defendants are part of a ring that committed many burglaries, sales of drugs, and generally any case where there are factors that make the case more serious than it appears on its face, or where the defendants have long records.

Where you are seeking a reduction to a misdemeanor and the case is one in which reductions are not standard operating procedure, you should discuss the matter with the arresting officer, marshal all the facts in your favor and then discuss the matter with the D.A. before court is in session or during a recess. In demonstration cases it is advisable to meet with the D.A. in charge of these cases in his office before the next court appearance. The defendant's past record and how he is presently occupying himself are of great importance. If the case is one which is impossible to win and you are certain that the defendant will be pleading guilty, informing the D.A. that there will be a plea can often lead to a reduction of even a serious case. The minor nature of the case, holes in the government's case, and any other mitigating factors should be pointed out to the D.A. in arguing for the reduction.

It may also be necessary to waive the preliminary hearing and even the right to a jury trial to get the reduction; this presents a very difficult problem. On the one hand, having the preliminary hearing may mean that the defendant will have to go to trial on a felony charge and, where there is a likelihood of a jail sentence, this increases the stakes enormously since the sentence can be high. On the other hand, not having the preliminary hearing may mean the loss of important discovery information before trial. I usually lean toward waiving the preliminary hearing for the reduction since other discovery devices can at least partially replace the hearing. Also, keeping the case in

Criminal Court makes it much more maneuverable and increases the chances of such things as dismissals for failure to prosecute (if the police officers fail to show up on several occasions) and being able to plead guilty before a relatively lenient judge. In Supreme Court the police officer does not have to appear unless the case is actually scheduled for trial so there are no dismissals due to his non-appearance, and in Supreme Court the prosecutor picks the judge before whom the case appears.

In felony cases where a plea is contemplated, and it appears that the D.A. will accept a plea to a misdemeanor in Criminal Court, the defendant has the option of pleading guilty in Criminal Court or, by waiting for an indictment, in Supreme Court. The decision should be based upon whether a jail sentence is likely, who is sitting in the Criminal Court part where the defendant will be sentenced, and whether any advantages can be gained by being able to bargain for sentence in Supreme Court (see Chapter 10). Note that if the case goes to Supreme Court the D.A. may insist on a plea to a felony, even where there will be no jail time, while the same case might be resolved in Criminal Court as a misdemeanor. Having a schedule of judges is important in making this decision. Often a lenient judge sits in Part 2B, the calendar part of the three-judge bench. A good tactic can be to get a reduction to a misdemeanor in Part 1D or 1D1 (which can be facilitated by promising the D.A. that there will be a plea), waiving the preliminary hearing, consenting to motions within trial, asking for a three-judge bench, and having the case adjourned to Part 2B, where your client can plead.

The courtroom procedure for a reduction is that, when the case is called, you discuss the matter with the D.A., if you have not already done so, and if you come to an agreement, he will then move to reduce the charges to a misdemeanor and give the court the applicable section of the Penal Law to which the charges are to be reduced. The judge will grant the motion and the court clerk will ask you if you waive the reading of the reduced charges and rights thereunder, to which you answer "yes," and then the case is handled as a misdemeanor. Under the new structure of the Criminal Court, the case does not have to be sent to another part and the next step in the case can take place immediately if all parties so desire.

Felony cases can be submitted to the grand jury at any time, and, after an indictment is handed down, the Criminal Court immediately loses jurisdiction. Several cases have held that an indictment causes the defendant to lose his right to a preliminary hearing. Normally you will not be told when the case will be presented to the grand jury, but you can prevent the case from being presented without your knowledge by serving notice upon the D.A.'s office and the foreman of the grand jury that the defendant desires to testify, or that the defendant wishes the grand jury to hear some other witness (§ 190.50 C.P.L.). Having the defendant testify is very risky since he must waive immunity and therefore anything he says can be introduced against him at trial, and the defense lawyer cannot be present in the grand jury room. Usually there is little or nothing to be gained from the defendant testifying, and the possible gains are not worth the risks except in unusual cases.

If you desire your client or some other witness to testify before the grand jury, all you have to do is notify the D.A.'s office and the foreman of the grand jury (address it to that title) by simple letter. It is then incumbent on him to notify you when the case is being presented and take care of any other details, such as getting your client from jail to the grand jury room. In borderline cases where the facts technically constitute a felony but an indictment may or may not be returned, submitting a character witness may tip the scales in favor of a misdemeanor. However, § 190.50(6) gives the grand jury the option of refusing to hear defense witnesses other than the defendant. Since the D.A. must read the name of the prospective witness before deciding whether to hear him or her, titles of character witnesses may be helpful. Note that misdemeanors, particularly in large demonstration cases where the District Attorney is trying to avoid preliminary hearings, are sometimes submitted to the grand jury in order to obtain informations and avoid preliminary hearings. Where you suspect that this may happen (attorneys who do a great deal of work in this area can usually tell you if the particular District Attorney in charge of demonstration cases is submitting them to the grand jury) you should consider sending a notice of intent to submit the defendant or other witnesses to the grand jury, to the District Attorney as soon after the arrest as possible. Your letter may cause him to change his mind about sending the case to the grand jury since, if his witnesses testify, you are entitled to the transcript of that testimony during trial for your cross-examination. § 230 of the old Code of Criminal Procedure, which gave the defense the right to voir dire the grand jury before the case was presented, has been deleted from the new law.

After an indictment comes down, the defendant is arraigned on the new felony charges in Part 30 if he is an adult or Part 31 if he is a youth. Defense counsel is notified by mail of the date of the arraignment. If the defendant is out on bail which was set while the case was in Criminal Court, it will almost definitely be continued. After a not guilty plea is entered in Part 30, the case is marked off calendar and about three weeks later it will appear on a trial calendar in one of the trial parts, again with notification to the defendant and counsel by mail. Cases in Part 31 remain there for trial. The handling of a felony case from this point on is beyond the scope of this book.

C. Interviewing Your Client

The lawyer who practices ordinary criminal law will quickly learn that a great many of his clients in non-political cases will claim their innocence and will actually be lying. It is important to get the truth from your client in order to properly evaluate the case and to avoid tactical errors. For example, if the true facts indicate not only that the defendant is guilty but that the case is not one that can be won, then your thinking should be directed toward winning a dismissal by some means other than a trial, or pleading guilty under favorable circumstances, instead of going to trial, losing, and getting time. Knowing the truth can also avoid the tactical error of submitting your client to a lie detector test in the District Attorney's office and having him fail it. These problems generally arise only in ordinary criminal cases rather than political cases.

A short speech in which you tell your client that most of the people you represent are actually guilty, that it is your job to defend the guilty as well as the innocent, that you will defend him to the limit of your ability even if he is guilty, that you will not make him plead guilty merely because he is in fact guilty, and that it is a mistake not to tell a lawyer the truth because the lawyer will make tactical mistakes to the defendant's disadvantage unless he knows the truth, is usually sufficient. If the story related to you still seems unbelievable, tell the defendant that you can probably win a dismissal by having him submit to a lie detector test administered by the District Attorney's office but that he should not take this test unless he will pass it, since if he flunks it they will prosecute with a vengeance. Your client's reaction to this statement will usually, but not always, bring out the truth. Many young people lie to their parents and are afraid of them, and it is a good practice to interview clients without their parents present.

At the initial interview with your client you should take down a detailed statement of the facts and you should also find out the defendant's prior record, his job or school situation, whether he has a drug problem and if so how bad it is, and whether he has psychiatric problems that he is aware of. Your efforts to get him to do something about himself should begin at the first interview. Of course, since lawyers are not psychiatrists or social workers they can do little more than refer their clients to other agencies but they can and should know something about what agencies and services are available and a lawyer's continuing and genuine interest in his client can itself be helpful. See Chapters 9 and 12 for a more detailed discussion of this subject.

D. Bench Warrants

When a defendant fails to appear his bail is forfeited or parole revoked and a bench warrant is issued. If a lawyer appears on the defendant's behalf at the time the case is called and tells the court that he knows the defendant and that he is confident that the defendant has failed to appear only because of an oversight, that the defendant is not evading the court processes and that he will appear on the next occasion, or that the defendant is ill or in jail, the bench warrant will probably be stayed until an adjourned date. Some judges will stay the bench warrant if the preliminary hearing is waived and the matter is sent to a trial part. The issuance of any previous bench warrants and the general bail facts about the defendant are important factors in deciding whether the bench warrant will be stayed. Where the warrant is stayed and the defendant appears on the adjourned date there will be no problem; the bench warrant will be vacated without much ado.

When a bench warrant is not stayed, the judge simply announces that the bail is forfeited or parole evoked, bench warrant to issue. The case is not adjourned to a particular date; it is off calendar. The defendant must come into the courthouse, surrender himself to the warrant squad (on the second floor in New York County) and he is then taken in custody to the jail part of the complex where the warrant was issued. That is, if the warrant was issued in Part 3 (the non-jail youth part) or Part AP7 (the non-jail felony part), defendant is arraigned on the warrant in Part 3A or AP1, respectively. All other parts 2A and 2B are both jail and non-jail parts so your client would be arraigned in whichever part issued the warrant. The judge who arraigns the defendant on the bench warrant can therefore be chosen to a limited extent by timing the surrender. The court papers are obtained and the case is added to the calendar for that day for the purposes of vacating the warrant, or setting new bail in some cases, and getting the case back on the calendar so the prosecution can continue. All the attorney has to do is turn the defendant in at the office of the Warrant Squad (7th Precinct, Delancey and Clinton Streets in New York County) and wait for his client to be brought to the proper part.

A bail forfeiture takes about three to four weeks to go through. Thus, if a defendant is arraigned on the warrant within this period of time, the court can order bail reinstated and your client will not lose his bail. The fact that a bail forfeiture has gone through is often not apparent on the court papers, and, provided that the clerk does not check the matter out and inform the court that the bail forfeiture is complete, a judge can note on the papers that the bail is reinstated and the defendant will be released from the courtroom even though in fact the bail has been forfeited. Where the time interval between the issuance of the warrant and arraignment on the warrant is long, and the bail is obviously forfeited, the court can set a new bail and the defendant will be held until it is posted.

Arraignment on a bench warrant means that the defendant is brought before the court, the warrant is automatically vacated, and the court decides to reinstate bail or parole, or to increase bail or, where bail has been forfeited, to set a new bail or parole the defendant. Where the defendant has a valid excuse such as illness (a note from a physician or hospital is decisive), or that he was given the wrong return date by his lawyer, or anything else that seems to be beyond the defendant's control, it is likely that he will be released from the court. A relevant factor is whether he came to court as soon as he was able. If bail has been forfeited, but the defendant has a very valid excuse, you should request parole on the ground that he has already been penalized by losing his bail money; and point out the fact that he has voluntarily surrendered himself as soon as he was able proves his reliability.

At the arraignment on the warrant, the lawyer should inform the court of the reason for his client's failure to appear, and he better have one. If it is a poor reason, counsel should also give the court the general bail facts about the defendant and he should tell the court that he is confident that the defendant will appear in the future. The fact that the defendant voluntarily surrendered himself should also be pointed out to the court. Of course, the court is very influenced by whether there have been bench warrants in the past.

Some judges, although not satisfied by a defendant's excuse, do not want to send him to jail and as an alternative they impose a fine of $25 or $50, which is allegedly to cover the court costs resulting from defendant's non-appearance. § 540.10 of the C.P.L. gives the court the right to place conditions of the reinstatement of bail, so such an action is apparently legal. If the defendant refuses to pay the court may then simply refuse to reinstate bail, or even raise the bail, and the defendant will go to jail. However, if the defendant cannot afford to pay then it should be argued that *Tate v. Short* 91 S. Ct. 668 (1971), in which the Supreme Court held that poor people who could not afford to pay a fine cannot be put in jail, makes it illegal to jail the defendant because he can't pay what amounts to a fine for lateness. However since the judge can simply refuse to reinstate bail instead of imposing a fine, it may be wiser to not argue against a fine but to ask the court to allow the defendant to pay next time he comes to court. It can then be asserted that the defendant does not have the money, and then the record will so clearly show that the defendant is being jailed because he is poor that the judge will have to rescind the fine. Obviously, your client could pay the court costs and sue for its return after the case is over.

The issuance of a bench warrant is damaging in a case where there is a possibility of a dismissal for failure to prosecute. When a complainant has failed to appear on several occasions and such a motion is made, the court examines the papers, and, if there has been a bench warrant in the past, the government will be given additional opportunities to produce the complainant. The reasons for this are that the court is generally reluctant to dismiss for failure to prosecute and uses the defendant's failure to appear as an excuse for postponing dismissal. Also, some defendants have learned that where the complainant fails to appear on the first two occasions and then appears on the third occasion, the defendant can increase his chances of making the complainant fail to show in the future by leaving the court on the occasion when he sees that the complainant is present.

Sometimes the issuance of bench warrants can be avoided entirely, that is, the matter can be adjourned without a bench warrant being issued and stayed, by furnishing documentary evidence of a valid excuse on the date of the non-appearance. When a person is rearrested and incarcerated in a New York City prison, a certificate showing incarceration can be obtained from the Department of Correction on the 14th floor of the Courthouse.

E. Bail Applications

An application for reduction of bail can be made at any stage of the proceedings, but only of course if the defendant is in jail. It can be made in Criminal Court any time the matter is before a judge in any part, and it can be made at any time in Part 31 of the Supreme Court. There are two types of bail: bond bail and cash bail. For example, bail may be set at $500 (bond) and there may or may not be a cash alternative of, say, $100. Thus your application can be to reduce the bond bail, to have a cash alternative set, or to lower the cash alternative that was previously set.

Note that cash can also be posted in the full amount of the bond bail, instead of buying a bond. If cash is posted instead of a bond, the city keeps 2 percent as a service charge. Bonds can be purchased at almost any hour from bondsmen who have storefront offices near the courthouse; they have large signs and cannot be missed. Bonds cost $50 per thousand for the first thousand dollars, $40 per thousand for the second thousand, and $30 per thousand thereafter. Thus a $500 bond costs $25, and a $1500 bond costs $70, etc. Generally, security in the amount of half the total value of the bond must be posted, and a guarantor who is employed must sign. The security can be in the form of cash, savings account bankbook, deed to a house, securities, etc.

In addition to the general bail facts about a defendant, which are discussed in the arraignment chapter and which should be pointed out to the court, there are many other factors that can persuade a judge to lower bail at a later stage of the proceedings. The case may have been reduced to a misdemeanor which in itself makes the bail excessive. There may have been several adjournments at the request of the state and the judge, after denying your motion to dismiss for failure to prosecute may want to do something for you by lowering bail. Where there have been delays and the defendant has spent a relatively long time in jail awaiting disposition of his case, that fact should be pointed out to the court. Where the defendant was an addict prior to arrest and he has shown an interest in getting into a drug program by writing to one, that fact should be pointed out. Where the inmate has actually been interviewed by a representative of a drug program and found acceptable, and if a representative of the program personally appears in court, most judges will, in not too heavy cases, parole the defendant to the custody of the program. However, parole is granted with the proviso that the D.A. must be notified if the defendant leaves the program, in which case parole will be revoked.

When making a bail application, as many people as possible should personally appear in court, and they should stand behind the rail while the case is before the court. Parents, interested aunts, uncles, older brothers and sisters, social workers, psychiatrists, counselors in settlement houses or other programs, and even employers can all be valuable in persuading a judge to reduce the bail. The court should be told exactly who is present in court and their relationship to the defendant, and that they are prepared to make a statement in support of the defendant. The judge will usually not ask for this. The court should be told what the defendant will be doing when he gets out of jail, where and with whom he will be living, whether he will be in school or working, and what programs he will be in. You should also tell the judge how much bail the defendant will be able to raise. Other arguments that can be made are that the bail exceeds the amounts usually set in similar cases, and you can cite other cases on the calendar of that day to show this; and, of course, you can argue denial of equal protection, that your client should not remain in jail just because he is poor, but such arguments have no effect.

If you cannot succeed in getting the bail lowered in Criminal Court, the matter is easily appealable to Supreme Court. Procedurally all that you have to do is fill out a short form, which you get from a court officer, in Part 31, and this can be done on any day. The court papers will be brought from the Criminal Court and you should then discuss the matter with the A.D.A. in Part 31. If you fill out the form before 11:30 A.M. the papers will be brought up by 12:30 P.M. and the D.A. will be able to meet with you at this time. You can have your client's relatives and allies meet you in Part 31 at that time. If you are able to reach an agreement with the D.A. you need go no further and the new bail will be noted on the court papers. If you cannot agree then you have the option of withdrawing the application or arguing the matter before the judge. You should not argue the matter unless you feel that, given the facts and circumstances of the case and the judge sitting, you have a good chance to succeed. The reason is that if you are not successful, the court papers will be endorsed "application for reduction in bail denied" and you will then have a difficult time getting the bail lowered in Criminal Court later on; withdrawing the application before arguing it before the judge will mean no notation on the court papers.

Chapter 5

DISMISSALS THROUGH PROGRAMS AND BY OTHER MEANS

A. Youth Counsel Bureau

The Youth Counsel Bureau (commonly known as Y.C.B.) is a counselling program for youths between 16 and 21 years of age who have no prior involvement with the law and at the conclusion of the counselling the case is dismissed. The procedure is as follows: The first time the case is on in court (in any part other than AR1) you simply request that the Youth Counsel Bureau be permitted to interview the defendant to determine his eligibility for admission into the program. Sometimes, if a case is of some political or community importance, preliminary negotiations with the D.A. and Y.C.B. before the court date can facilitate matters and the case can be accepted by Y.C.B. right away. The District Attorney must agree before a referral can be made, and in a borderline case it may be advisable to speak to the D.A. in private while court is not in session, either before the judge enters or during a break. If the D.A. does not oppose the referral, the judge will almost always go along with it. Unless there have been preliminary negotiations with Y.C.B., the case is then adjourned for a month or so for the Youth Counsel Bureau to report whether the case is acceptable to them and the complainant is excused for the next appearance. The complainant, defendant, defendant's parents or relatives, and you then go to the Y.C.B. office for an interview. If Y.C.B. decides to accept the case, they will so inform the court the next time the case is on the calendar. The matter is further adjourned for a period of three months during which time the defendant goes approximately every two weeks for counselling with a social worker. If the defendant makes all his appointments and agrees to mend his ways, the case is dismissed on the adjourned date.

No other services, such as psychiatric services or job training, are directly available through Y.C.B. It is, however, a fairly painless way of getting a case dismissed and should be used whenever possible, except for very political clients for whom there is a strong possibility of arrest during the counseling period. Any arrest before the case is dismissed will result in Y.C.B. withdrawing from the case. For many political clients an early plea to a violation, especially with a waiver of prints, is often a better result.

Individuals are eligible for the Y.C.B. program when they have no prior involvement with the law, when they are between 16 and 21 at the time of arrest, and when charges are relatively light. In very exceptional cases, with a letter to the D.A. in charge of Y.C.B., you may be able to get someone a few years over 21 into the program. The defendant need not be living with his parents, although if he is very young Y.C.B. will look upon him more favorably if he is. Parents or guardians should accompany youths to court in general, but particularly if Y.C.B. is being sought. Some examples of cases which are almost always acceptable to Y.C.B. are shoplifting, violations, small amounts of marijuana (but can be over the felony weight of ¼ ounce), small amounts of amphetamines and barbiturates, 3rd degree assault not against a police officer, and unauthorized use of a motor vehicle, particularly for passengers. They will generally not accept any but the lightest demonstration cases but sometimes pressure on the D.A. from government officials and politicians with some stature has helped moderately light demonstration cases, even where there were some felony charges, make it into Y.C.B. They will also generally not accept cases involving alleged offenses against police officers unless the officer, and sometimes even his commanding officer, agree. Y.C.B. does not accept heroin, hypodermic instruments ("works"), or LSD cases.

As far as the court is concerned, the decision of the Youth Counsel Bureau in accepting or rejecting a case is final and not reviewable by the court. If you feel that your client has been wrongfully denied acceptance by Y.C.B., the only recourse is to appeal to superiors of Y.C.B. and then, since Y.C.B. is under the supervision of the D.A.'s office, to the Assistant District Attorney in charge of the Criminal Court Bureau, or, in a very big case, to the District Attorney himself. Your best argument is that similar cases have been accepted by Y.C.B. in the past and it is a denial of equal protection to refuse your client at this time. If this fails you can note your objections on the record at the next court appearance for a possible, but weak, appealable issue.

B. The Manhattan Court Employment (Vera) Project

This is another program run somewhat under the auspices of the court which leads to eventual dismissal of the charges. Its official title is Manhattan Court Employment Project but it is commonly referred to as Vera since the Vera Institute of Justice developed the program and runs it. Vera's own rules are that only male defendants between 17 and 45 years of age, who are unemployed or underemployed (not earning over $125 per week), who have not spent more than a total of 6 months in jail (this is somewhat flexible on a case by case basis), who have no prior hard drug arrests, and who do not have serious mental problems, are eligible for the program. All charges are eligible except serious felonies (homicide, rape, robbery and certain others), hard drugs, violations, and certain other offenses such as gambling and traffic violations. If the defendant is on probation, the consent of his probation officer is required. The defendant can have no more than one other pending case, but if both cases are felonies, he is not eligible.

The procedure for getting someone into the Vera Project is as follows: Early in the morning go to the clerk's office of Part 3A on the second floor or call 732-0076, extension 40, and tell the people from Vera that you have a client whom you would like to have interviewed to see if he is eligible for the program. They will send a screener to interview him and if he seems acceptable to the screener, he will call a representative to further interview him and give final approval. You, the screener, and the police officer or complaining witness should then speak to the D.A. who has been assigned to these matters, before the case is called, in order to get his approval. The screener will know which D.A. is in charge of Vera and where to find him. If the case is called before the interviews are completed, have the defendant ask for a second call. When the case is called and you are ready, simply inform the court that the defendant has been interviewed and found acceptable by the Manhattan Court Employment Project, that the District Attorney approves, and that you therefore request a three-month adjournment for purposes of participation in this program. In cases of defendants with past records, know your judge, by asking the Legal Aid attorney if necessary, before attempting this; there are judges who will not, despite D.A. approval, allow a dismissal through Vera for a man with a prior record and the papers may be marked "Vera denied," which will prevent you from getting him admitted into Vera before any other judge. If the judge is bad, either have the case sent into a back-up part by having it marked ready for a hearing, or try for Vera next time the case is on.

In addition to fulfilling Vera's criteria, both the D.A. and the judge must consent to the referral. The charges or the defendant's past record may be such that either the D.A. or the judge refuse to agree to a dismissal through participation in the Vera project. There are no fixed guidelines and the decision is made on a case by case basis, with gut reactions being the most important factor. In a problem case, the lawyer should stress whatever favorable factors exist about the case and the defendant, and his skill as a salesman can be decisive. Such cases as possession of marijuana, small thefts, criminal possession of stolen property, third degree assault on a civilian, unauthorized use of a motor vehicle and possession of weapons other than guns, where the defendant's record is light, are generally readily acceptable by Vera and the D.A. More difficult, but possible, are first offenders in heavier crimes such as forgery, purse snatchings without violence, burglary, and possession of a pistol. In a pistol case where the D.A. denied Vera because of suspicions that defendant may be a robber, and your client swears that he is not, you may be able to gain him acceptance into Vera by submitting him to a private lie detector test. Lie detection services are listed in the yellow pages. Vera can enroll defendants who are in jail; if this happens, it means that at the time the court adjourns the case for three months for the purpose of the defendant participating in the Vera program, the defendant will be paroled to Vera.

The program of the Manhattan Court Employment Project consists of helping the man find as good a job as possible in his circumstances, and in providing excellent individual and group counselling. The defendant is required to attend group counselling-therapy sessions once per week, and he receives individual counselling depending on his circumstances. It should be noted that over half the people initially enrolled in the Vera project are terminated unfavorably from the program for various reasons, such as refusing to work or failure to attend the counselling sessions. Often, after the three-month adjournment, the Vera counsellor feels that the defendant should spend more time in the program and on the return date following the initial three-month adjournment, Vera requests a further adjournment, which is readily granted. Unfavorable termination from the program, although it should not have any effect at all, can have serious consequences. The court papers will be endorsed "Vera terminated" and this may prevent any further breaks you are seeking for the defendant and, if noticed, may adversely affect the sentence. The lawyer should therefore try to make certain that his client is really interested in participating in the program before he tries to get him enrolled.

C. Drug Programs for Drug Addicts

For addicts, whether or not they have been found to be addicts in the examination following arrest (see Chapter 9) the best way of avoiding incarceration and possibly of avoiding a criminal record is for him or her to become a resident of a drug treatment program. There are many such programs available in New York City, such as Odyssey House, Phoenix House, Daytop Village, etc., but they are overcrowded and difficult to get into.

Suffice it to say at this point that for first offenders or persons with light records, especially where the charge is only possession of the drugs, participation in a drug program for varying periods of time, averaging about a year depending on the program, can lead to dismissal of the charges. This topic is covered in greater detail in Chapter 9. The present policy of the D.A.'s office seems to be that even where a defendant is successfully participating in a program, they want a plea of guilty for the record and they say they will consent to or even recommend probation. Occasionally, however, for the young person with no record, there can be an agreement to a three or four-month adjournment for the purpose of submitting progress reports from the drug treatment program, with a view toward eventual dismissal. If the D.A. insists on a plea, and the defendant has participated in a program for a long time, you should push for a plea to a violation, such as loitering, so that the defendant does not have a record of a conviction of a crime, and so that the sentence can be a conditional discharge instead of probation (a sentence of probation cannot be imposed on a violation conviction).

D. Commitment to Mental Institutions

Long term commitment to a mental institution will often result in dismissal of the charges on motion of the Assistant District Attorney. The procedure is simply to get a letter from the mental institution and present it to the D.A. and the court and request a dismissal. Sometimes the court or the D.A. will want to make sure that the defendant spends some time there before the charges are dismissed so the case will be adjourned for three to six months and then dismissed.

This is not to suggest that commitment be considered to avoid jail since, for most mental institutions, the two are not far apart. In any event, that decision is not yours; it is mentioned here because it might happen to one of your clients.

E. Entry into the Armed Services

Some defendants, particularly those who are not politically aware and who are nowhere in their own lives, are desirous of joining the Armed Services. The problem is that the Army will not accept anyone who has any obligation to a court, including being on probation or even getting a conditional discharge, which in theory is in effect for one year from the date of sentencing. On the other hand, the court, predictably, would like to see more people joining the army but will not dismiss the case unless the man is already in the army; but he cannot join while the case is pending. Catch 22?!

A possible solution is as follows. Have your client sign up, take all the necessary physical and mental tests, and on request, he will be given a letter saying that he is scheduled for induction on a certain date if he is free of the court obligation. A few days before that date, have the case put on the calendar, bring your

46

client and his family to court, tell the court that you will personally escort him to induction, and ask the court for dismissal conditioned on his induction. There is no provision in the law for a conditional dismissal but the dismissal can be without prejudice to reopen and you can promise the judge that you will furnish proof of induction and that you will consent to reopen the case if the defendant is not actually inducted. Remember, however, that the transcript which shows the disposition of the case must read simply that the case is dismissed, not conditionally dismissed. If the court will not go along with this, perhaps you can get a plea to a violation and an unconditional discharge. A persuasive argument for getting an unconditional discharge is to inform the court that the defendant will not be able to join the army unless he is given an unconditional discharge; the army considers a conditional discharge to be an obligation to the court and they will refuse to accept a man until the condition expires after one year.

The above procedure will not work for heavy cases, particularly those involving violence, but it may work for cases as heavy as possession of heroin. Your argument is that since the purpose of the prosecution is to rehabilitate, the prosecution should be discontinued since the defendant is showing the court that he is drastically altering his life style.

F. Lie Detector Tests

Although the results of lie detector tests are not admissible in evidence at trial, the D.A. will often dismiss a case based upon the results of a lie detector test, unless there is other strong evidence showing that the test is inaccurate. It is often the only way out of a robbery charge in which there is one complaining witness and one defendant and there is no evidence other than the complainant's identification of the defendant, and the defendant's denial. Of course, the dismissal on motion of the D.A. also depends on the defendant's prior record, general background, and all other factors in the case. It can be used however in any kind of case. One problem is that the New York County District Attorney's Office has only one lie detector specialist and he must therefore be used sparingly.

When in doubt about whether your client will pass a lie detector test, you can submit him to a private test before telling the D.A. that your client is willing to submit to a lie detector test. The fee for such a test is approximately $150.

G. Dismissals in the Interest of Justice

Sections 170.30, 170.40, and 170.55 provide for dismissals in the interest of justice and adjournments in contemplation of dismissal, without setting forth guidelines for such dismissals. These sections authorize the dismissal of cases that have no defects in them and could lead to conviction, and the dismissal can be for any reason. A motion for dismissal in the interest of justice can be made by a defense attorney, but few judges will grant such a motion over an Assistant District Attorney's opposition. When making such a motion you should therefore concentrate your attention on persuading the D.A. that a dismissal is warranted. An adjournment in contemplation of dismissal (formerly called a dismissal on recognizance, or D. O. R.) means that the case is adjourned without a date being set, that the state can, on motion, reopen the case within six months, and that if the state does not reopen the case within six months, it is deemed to have been dismissed in furtherance of justice. The prosecutor must consent to an adjournment in contemplation of dismissal.

Such dismissals are generally obtainable only when the case is very minor, such as smoking in the subway or possession of marijuana, or the state's evidence is weak, or the defendant is in some kind of rehabilitative program. In small heroin cases, where the defendant has a light record, an adjournment in contemplation of dismissal can often be obtained when the defendant is in a methadone or residential treatment program. Another possibility is that if your client has just started in the program the D.A. may agree to an adjournment to a specific date with an informal agreement that he will adjourn in contemplation of dismissal on that date if the defendant is still in the drug program. You should make sure that such agreements are noted on your file with the A.D.A.'s name, and on the prosecutor's file. Of course the availability of this type of dismissal depends very much on which Assistant District Attorney is in the part at the time. The Legal Aid lawyers can help you if you do not know the particular A.D.A. and, unless a specific A.D.A. is assigned to the case, it may be advantageous to discuss dismissal in another part or on another day.

Chapter 6

PRELIMINARY HEARINGS AND OTHER DISCOVERY DEVICES

A. Preliminary Hearings

A preliminary hearing is a hearing in which the State must present to the court a prima facie case. Usually the government has its witness or witnesses take the stand and their entire case is presented and you have the opportunity to cross examine. As a discovery device it is, obviously, unsurpassable. You learn almost the government's entire case and what the witnesses are like. The preliminary hearing also serves the important function of pinning the witness' testimony down. The minutes of the hearing can be used to impeach at trial and also to bring out inconsistencies between different witnesses. The advantages of preliminary hearings are so great that they should never be waived unless (1) it is a serious case and you are offered a reduction to a misdemeanor in return for waiving the preliminary hearing and the defendant would otherwise be indicted (see Chapter 4B) or (2) you have reason to believe that the witness is very old and might die, or might move out of state and be unavailable for trial, and the preliminary hearing would serve to perpetuate his testimony. See CPL Article 660. Note that the minutes of the preliminary hearing are not admissible at trial unless the state proves that the witness is out of state, or sick, or dead, or insane. If the witness disappears or cannot be found, the deposition is not admissible.

Surprisingly, the new Criminal Procedure Law, even though it was drafted entirely by prosecutors, still permits preliminary hearings for persons accused of misdemeanors in New York City

(§ 170.75). Persons accused of felonies, including youths, are entitled to preliminary hearings unless there has been an indictment. Any grand jury action, including the return of an information on a misdemeanor, precludes a preliminary hearing since the theoretical purpose of a preliminary hearing is for the court to determine whether the case should be held for trial. The return of an indictment or information by the grand jury is deemed to be a decision by a superior court that the matter should be tried. As mentioned in Chapter 4B, in large demonstration arrests the D.A.'s office has in the past prevented preliminary hearings by obtaining informations from the grand jury. If you suspect that this may happen, you should have your hearing right away or at least make sure that you will be notified when the case will be submitted to the grand jury, either by requesting to voir dire or submitting witnesses to the grand jury. See Chapter 4B.

In certain kinds of felonies, the District Attorney's office, with the full complicity of the courts, systematically seeks adjournments so that there will be an indictment without a preliminary hearing. This occurs most notably in homicides and sales of drugs to undercover agents, where the complaint is on a short affidavit; the government does not even have its witnesses appear in Criminal Court. If you can locate the witnesses, you can subpoena them yourself. If your client is in jail, § 180.80 of the C.P.L. provides that the defendant must be released from custody if a hearing is not held within 72 hours of arrest, unless the delay is at the defendant's request, or is consented to, or the D.A. can show good cause (not defined) for permitting a further delay. If the judge allows a longer delay, you should request that the papers be marked "final against the state for a preliminary hearing," referred to as "final markings." When a case is marked "final" this means that if the state cannot go forward on the next date the case is on the calendar, it should be dismissed upon a defense motion to dismiss for failure to prosecute, although many judges will not dismiss despite final markings. You can also challenge the continued detention by bringing habeas corpus proceedings in Supreme Court. In the past, efforts like this were almost never successful; the courts were aware of the fact that the D.A.'s office was intentionally avoiding hearings and they sanctioned the practice. With the new law the courts may be more receptive, at least to releasing an arrestee until a hearing is held. Keep in mind that if someone is released and a hearing is held at a later date, or an indictment comes down, bail may be reimposed and the defendant will go back to jail. In serious cases such as homicides and drug sales to under-cover agents bail will almost certainly be reimposed after an indictment or hearing.

Of course, in any felony case which the District Attorney intends to submit to grand jury, you will lose your preliminary hearing if you delay long enough. The general practice is that the complainants do not arrange to submit the case to the grand jury until told to do so by the D.A. in the part where the case is on the calendar. You can sometimes overhear the D.A. telling the officer to go right to the grand jury while the case is before the court on a calendar call, in which case you better have your hearing that day if you can. On the other hand if the case is called and adjourned and the officer is not told to go to the grand jury, then you can be fairly certain that there will not be an indictment before the next court date. You can, of course, ask the officer about this.

The magic words for obtaining a preliminary hearing are: "defendant is ready for a preliminary hearing." The hearing will be heard either in a back-up part, on a first come, first served basis, or in the calendar part after the calendar is finished, generally in the afternoon. When it is called in the morning you can have it marked ready for 2:00 P.M. and leave the court until then. Although in the past the courts were often not able to hear all the cases marked ready, under the new system if the part the case is in has too many cases, the case is simply sent to another part and generally all cases marked ready are reached.

In cross examining at a preliminary hearing, the key word, as in all cross, is detail. For those without too much experience, it may be helpful to write out the questions. Probably the easiest method is to take notes during the complainant's testimony and to chronologically, from a time preceding to a time following the events he has related, take him through his testimony, directing your questions to all the details of his story that you can think of. You should bring out factors such as distances, positions, time intervals, all the exact words spoken, step by step narrative of movements, blow by blow details of fights, surrounding circumstances such as other people, buildings, noise, lighting, etc. Your questions should be such that you could, from the answers, make a sound moving picture of the occurrence. Of course, the questioning depends on the case. Before conducting the hearing, be sure to read the section of the statute the defendant is accused of violating and question on all elements of the crime. Other than that, the questioning depends on common sense. For example, where your client was a passenger in a stolen car and he is charged with unauthorized use of a motor vehicle, and your defense at trial will be lack of knowledge that the car was stolen, relevant questions are the general condition and age of the car, whether the ignition was torn out or whether there was a key in the ignition, whether any windows or the trunk had been broken in, etc.

At the preliminary hearing you should also investigate, as much as the court will allow, *Miranda* and *Wade* factors, search questions, etc. (see Chapter 7). Your object should be to bring out all the facts about questioning, statements, an identification, a search, etc., in order to prepare yourself for a hearing on a motion and in order to freeze the officer's testimony. The problem is that the District Attorney will object to such probing on the grounds that it is not relevant to a preliminary hearing, where all that the State must show is enough evidence to make out a prima facie case. Many judges will sustain the objections and limit your questioning. Your arguments in opposition to the objection can be (1) that the question relates to the actual commission of the crime (i.e. questions about a search relate to the circumstances of the possession itself) or, (2) that the State must show at a preliminary hearing that the case should be tried; if there are obvious search or *Miranda* defects which will mean eventual dismissal, that dismissal should take place after the preliminary hearing (there are numerous unreported Criminal Court cases in which such dismissals took place), and, (3) that the CPL (§ 180.60) does not put a limitation on the right to cross-examine.

Intent is also a necessary element in many cases and evidence showing intent should be adduced. For example, in a preliminary hearing of a case in which defendant was charged with criminal possession of stolen property, the evidence showed that the defendant pawned the item under his own name and address (note hearsay not objected to), and that he went voluntarily to see the detective who had left a message for him to

52

call; case dismissed after preliminary hearing without defendant taking the stand because the evidence clearly showed lack of intent.

In demonstration cases, as in many other cases where the police officer is the complainant, your main methods of discrediting his testimony are by showing that parts of it are contradictory or impossible, and by subpoenaing other police officers and letting them contradict each other, which they often do. That is one of the reasons for attention to detail. You should also ask the arresting officer at the preliminary hearing for the names and shield numbers of other officers present at the scene. The court may not permit this question at the preliminary hearing on the ground that it is not relevant to the question of whether the case should be held for trial. If this happens, simply request that the names of other witnesses be furnished to defense counsel as possibly exculpatory evidence, and tell the court that if this is not furnished at this time, it will be requested in a bill of particulars or motion for discovery at the next court appearance and necessitate a continuance of the trial for the production of those witnesses. For some case law on the right of the defendant to such evidence, see section C of this chapter.

In cases where there are many defendants, or in any other case where you suspect that the police officer or complaining witness cannot identify the defendant, the preliminary hearing is the place to demonstrate this. As in the arraignment, instruct your clients to remain seated while the case is being called and move to exclude the complainant during the calendar call. If this motion is denied then move that the complainant be instructed to face the other way. Your argument should be that any future identification will be permanently tainted by this identification and that, if the trial court rules that that has happened, then no identification evidence will be admissible and the government will have to prove its case by evidence other than identification. The court may smell a possible loss of a conviction and grant your motion.

Showing inability to identify can be done by asking the complainant whether he knows which defendant is named so and so, one by one until all defendants are named. You can also ask which of the defendants he recognizes as having been at the scene of arrest (this will suggest to him that he doesn't recognize them all). Of those that he recognizes, ask him where they were in relation to the others and in relation to objects at the scene of arrest. Of course, the police can identify defendants also, and they have learned to avoid losing cases through non-identification by having enough arresting officers so that each one can remember his arrestees. In some cases the police even photograph each defendant at the site of the arrest or in the police station.

Where the complainant is a civilian, and the encounter at the time of arrest was very brief, and the station house identification was doubtful or improper, and the complainant has not seen the defendant for a long time, and you suspect that the complainant may not be able to identify the defendant or defendants, you can seek an in-court identification. At the calendar call, have your client remain seated, advise the court that the defendant is in the courtroom, that previous identifications were improper due to lack of a line-up and lack of counsel, and ask that the complainant identify the defendant in open court. Of course, the arresting officer must be forbidden to advise the complainant. Obviously, this tactic stands more of a chance of success if your client is average looking, and there are others in the courtroom who fit his description, and the courtroom is crowded. Asking for such an identification in the Criminal Court is very irregular and many judges will deny the request and perhaps holler a little.

If the state has more than one witness to present at the preliminary hearing, be sure to move to exclude all witnesses other than the one testifying. After testifying, each witness should be asked to leave the room on the ground that witnesses should not be permitted to hear the testimony of other witnesses prior to trial.

The new law (§ 180.60) gives the court discretionary power to grant or deny a defense request to call other witnesses, but any witness that you call should be a prosecution witness. You can call other police officers present at the scene or private citizens who are witnesses to the occurrence. Where you are trying to show that the police officer is lying, such a tactic may be helpful, and, if you do not have the names of such persons prior to the hearing, you can even get a continuance of the

54

hearing after the state has presented its side of the case. Sometimes the arresting officer's partner will be in the courtroom and you will be able to call him as a witness without advance notice to him and the officers may not have had a chance to prepare the story together. In large mass arrests the tactic of having a very long preliminary hearing has on rare occasion led to the state accepting a plea to a violation where such a plea would otherwise not have been offered.

The defendant has the right to make a sworn or unsworn statement, at his option, at the preliminary hearing, and he is not subject to cross-examination. It is rare that such a tactic serves any purpose, since the court will hold the case for trial when the testimony of the government's witnesses makes out a crime, and it may help the D.A. prepare his case for trial.

The standard motion by defense counsel at the close of a preliminary hearing is: "defendant moves to dismiss for failure of the state to show a prima facie case." The court will then, if it denies the motion, ask how the defendant pleads and whether the defendant wants a one- or three-man bench or a jury. If you desire to have a hearing on a motion, your answer is that the defendant does not plead at this time and requests an adjournment to the same part for a hearing on a motion. Occasionally, the court will invoke C.P.L. § 710, 40–3, which says that upon the D.A.'s request, the court must order that the hearing be held within trial. Since this is obviously illegal (see Chapter 7), upon your objection the trial part will probably send the matter back to the motion part and all that is lost is time. Where a jury trial will be held, the court may send the case to a jury part (unless it is in the MAP Part, in which case it stays there), and the hearing on the motion will be held separately from the trial, before the trial judge.

B. Conversations with Witnesses

The most useful discovery device, other than a preliminary hearing, is often an informal conversation with the police officer or civilian complainant. Where the complainant is a civilian or where there are other civilian witnesses, you should not hesitate to visit them at their home in the evening. Of course, the witness does not have to speak to you but if you are polite and you act as though you are merely seeking the truth (possibly for deciding whether the defendant should plead guilty) and if you explain to him that you as a lawyer for the defense are completely authorized to speak to all witnesses, and that you would be remiss in your job if you did not, you may be able to open him up. If you are a male, it may be helpful to bring along a female law associate or secretary, since people seem to be less afraid to talk to a strange man who is with a woman; it is also helpful to have someone with you to act as a witness to the statements made. In the event that the statement given to you differs from the testimony of the witnesses in court, it is better to impeach that testimony (by a prior inconsistent statement) by having someone else rather than yourself testify since you will appear to be more partisan. Another technique for getting reluctant witnesses to speak to you is to say that your client said such and such and ask whether that is true. People take this as somewhat of an accusation that they are lying and they are tempted to defend themselves by opening up and giving their side of the story.

Incidentally, prosecutors and judges are occasionally under the misapprehension that defense lawyers are for some reason not free to speak to prosecution witnesses. Not only is it completely proper for defense attorneys to talk to any witness (see canon 39 of the Canons of Professional Ethics), but it has even been held that it is improper for the prosecutor to instruct witnesses not to talk to the defendant's attorney. *Gregory v. United States*, 369 F.2d 185 (USCADC 1966). Of course, if the prosecutor has already so instructed the witnesses your only remedy would be to seek a court order directing that the prosecutor rescind his instructions and refrain from such acts in the future, but the damage may already have been done.

Where the complainant is a police officer, he should also be spoken to. However, your interview should be very informal, either inside the courtroom or out in the hall. One posture that often gets them to open up is that you agree that there is something wrong with the defendant; and you want to do something to rehabilitate him, but you want to know if the case is really serious. Many police officers will refuse to talk to you at all and the only thing that may open them up is a mild threat that the case will be dragged on interminably with a preliminary hearing, a motion for a bill of particulars, and a motion for discovery, which can all be avoided if the officer just tells you briefly what happened. Of course, if you know the police officer is lying and if you know what his story will be (e.g.: a dropsey story), then talking to him is of little benefit.

C. Bills of Particulars and Motions for Discovery

An example of a motion for a bill of particulars is contained in the appendix, page 146. Bills of particulars are authorized by 200.90 and 100.45 of the C.P.L., which state that they are available when necessary to enable the defendant to conduct his defense, and the reason for the necessity must be given in the supporting affidavit. Its primary usefulness is in a complicated felony case where the indictment has general language or where there are charges against more than one defendant but it is not clear what each defendant is accused of doing. In such cases a bill of particulars may serve to limit the proof introduced by the state at trial. For finding out details about how the crimes were allegedly committed or for discovering other evidence, other discovery devices are definitely more useful, although if and when preliminary hearings for misdemeanors are abolished, bills of particulars may become more important.

Article 240 of the new C.P.L. contains guidelines for motions for discovery, which previously were based on case law. Section 240.10(3) bars the defense from obtaining internal police memos or reports but it should be argued that this section is unconstitutional. A motion for discovery can seek such evidence as reports from undercover agents, tapes and logs of conversations overheard through telephone taps and electronic surveillance, names of witnesses, etc. See pages 147 to 155 for sample motion papers. If your motion is complicated, it should be supported by a brief, which you can begin researching for by reading *Brady v. Maryland*, 373 U.S. 83 (1963), and, for interesting dicta, *Giles v. Maryland*, 386 U.S. 66 (1967).

The language of the Supreme Court in Brady seems to provide for broad discovery: "We now hold that the suppression by the prosecution of evidence favorable to an accused upon request violates due process where the evidence is material either to guilt or to punishment, irrespective of the good faith or bad faith of the prosecution." Such motions for discovery should therefore be made for any material or facts which you believe might be helpful to the defendant, such as evidence which tends to impugn the testimony of a prosecution witness (his prior criminal record or evidence indicating mental instability), scientific reports, etc. When making such a motion, it should be argued that the requested materials should be given to the defendant immediately, not at trial. *United States v. Gleason*, 265 F. Supp. 880 (S.D.N.Y. 1967). It should also be argued that the defendant's lawyer should be the one to decide what is or is not useful to the defendant in proving his or her innocence. *Dennis v. United States*, 384 U.S. 855 (1966).

The mechanics of making all motions are to serve motion papers on the Clerk of the District Attorney five or more days prior to the date the case is on the calendar. Have him stamp the original "copy received," and then serve the original on the clerk of the part in which the case is pending. In motions of this type, the supporting affidavit can be by the defendant or his attorney.

D. Subpoena Powers for Witnesses & Records

The attorney for the defendant has the power to subpoena any individual and any record or document, without court approval, with the exception that a subpoena duces tecum (for records, documents, etc.) directed to a government agency must be signed by a judge. Articles 610 to 650 of the Criminal Procedure Law. The rules governing service of subpoenas are contained in the Civil Practice Law and Rules, sections 2303 and 308. Simply summarized, they state that subpoenas must be personally served at any time prior to trial and the witness must be paid a fee of two dollars plus round trip transportation costs. If personal service is not possible the subpoena can be served by what is called "substituted service," described in CPLR § 308. The fees are waived by many government agencies and by police officers. Subpoenas on police officers will usually be obeyed when they are left with the desk officer of the precinct to which he is assigned.

Blank subpoena forms for witnesses can be obtained in one of the clerk's offices. Subpoenas duces tecum are usually prepared on Blumberg forms, which are available at stationery stores near courthouses. The way to get them signed is to bring them to the clerk's office of the part where the case is pending, have him pull the court papers; and usually you will be able to go right before the judge and have the subpoena signed on the spot.

Police Department records which are routinely prepared in every case can be obtained by use of a subpoena duces tecum. The subpoena must be served on the Police Department Information Unit, located at 400 Broome Street, New York, New York. The records will be produced on the return date of the subpoena, which need not be the date the case actually goes to trial, in the clerk's office of the part where the case is on the calendar. You will be able to examine the documents simply by asking the clerk for them and, if they are not helpful to your case, they need not be used. A little known record that can be very useful is a book kept in the police station that has a list of arrestees and the charges against them when they are first brought in to the precinct house. There is also a record of the time of arrest.

As for memorandum books, police officers often fail to bring them to court for the trial and it may be necessary to serve the officer with a subpoena duces tecum. This little chore can be avoided by asking the judge after the conclusion of the preliminary hearing to instruct the police officer to bring his memorandum book to court on every subsequent appearance he makes in the case. You will not be permitted to see his memorandum book until after he testifies, and then, theoretically, only for the purpose of using it as a prior inconsistent statement which impeaches his testimony.

Limited additional discovery can be gotten by subpoenaing various hospital records, Bureau of Motor Vehicle Records, store records, etc. Occasionally records of private complainants may be useful, such as the rent records of an apartment in which the defendant was arrested and charged with criminal trespass; if the landlord cannot show a termination of the most recent lessee's tenancy (and that means more than simply non-payment of rent), then the landlord cannot be the complainant in a criminal trespass charge.

E. Free Transcripts of Proceedings

Section 302 of the Judiciary Law gives an indigent defendant

59

the right to a free transcript of any proceedings in a criminal case. Thus, wherever necessary, you should obtain the minutes of a preliminary hearing prior to a motion to suppress, and the minutes of hearings on motions prior to trial.

The procedure for obtaining free transcripts is simply to make a motion at any time in the part where the case is pending. The motion papers consist of a proposed order and a supporting affidavit by the defendant in which he states that he needs the minutes of the proceeding in order to prepare for trial and that he cannot afford to buy the minutes. The defendant's affidavit should also contain a summary of the defendant's financial condition, including his income, number of dependents, rent, and amount of money in the bank (see Appendix, page 144).The motion can be made at any time but it should be made shortly after the proceeding for which you are seeking minutes since, if the court reporter is busy, it may take him some time to prepare them. The procedure is to serve a copy of the motion papers on the District Attorney's clerk's office five or more days prior to the return date of the motion and then to give the original to the clerk in the part where the case is pending. You can give the motion papers to the clerk on the return date of the motion and he will simply bring the motion papers and the court papers to the judge and the judge will probably sign the order on the spot. You should then conform a copy and serve it on the court reporter.

Court reporters ordinarily charge $1.25 per page for minutes but they receive only $.50 per page when the city pays for them. Thus if you have obtained a court order for a free transcript, you may have to wait until the court reporter has completed some of the cases for which he is being paid a full fee; if you need a transcript in a hurry you may have to pay for it.

Chapter 7

MOTION PRACTICE

A. Introduction

The four motions on which hearings are commonly held in Criminal Court are motions to suppress the evidence on the ground that it was obtained through an illegal search, motions to controvert search warrants, motions to suppress statements made by the defendant on the ground that they were illegally obtained (commonly called *Huntley* Hearings, *People vs. Huntley*, 15 N.Y.2d 72 [1965]), and motions to suppress identifications (called *Wade* hearings, *U.S. v. Wade*, 388 U.S. 218 [1967]). These hearings are often the most important proceedings in the case; for many cases winning or losing the motion determines the outcome of the case. Hearings on motions demand as much preparation as a trial, including a thorough factual investigation, preparation on the law, and preparation of your witnesses. You should have the minutes of the preliminary hearing, you should prepare your direct and cross-examination, and you should know what the general thrust of your arguments will be in order to respond to objections and to make a forceful summation. This chapter will briefly outline the law in each area, and an attempt will be made to describe the most common factual situations you will run into, together with suggested tactics. For a more thorough analysis you are referred to an excellent book, to which I am indebted, *Law and Tactics in Exclusionary Hearings*, by Thomas P. Abbott & others (Coiner Pub. Ltd., Wash., D.C. [1969]).

All motions should be made after there has been a preliminary hearing and the hearing on the motion should be separate from the trial. Section 710.40(3) of the CPL provides that in

Criminal Court only, the judge must, upon request of the D.A., order the motion to be held within trial. Particularly on motions based on illegal searches, defendant should object to this on the grounds that it violates (1) defendant's rights against self-incrimination, since if the suppression hearings were separate the defendant could testify that the contraband was in his possession and this testimony would not be admissible at trial; and (2) due process, since hearsay is admissible on motions to suppress but not at trial. If the judge at the preliminary hearing orders the motion to be held within trial and you renew your objection prior to trial, the three-man bench will usually send the case back to the motion part. If it does not, then you have probably guaranteed a reversal on appeal if you lose the trial, although it apparently has not been tested yet. Where the case is sent to the jury trial part, the hearing on the motion is held in that part, but before trial.

All motions should be made on papers, although the courts are not uniformly strict in requiring that there be formal papers. The papers are short, easy to prepare, and need not be overly specific and, since papers formalize the proceedings somewhat, it is generally advisable to prepare motion papers. See Appendix, page 156, for a sample.

Police lying, particularly on motions to suppress based on illegal searches and at *Huntley* hearings, is rampant and you should be prepared for it. Where applicable you should subpoena police reports and other officers who were present at the time of arrest, and the arresting officer should be instructed to have his memorandum book with him. You should prepare a close detailed cross-examination.

B. Motions to Suppress Evidence on the Ground It Was Obtained as a Result of an Illegal Search and Seizure (But Without a Warrant)

This motion can be made when the government intends to introduce contraband or any other evidence against your client. The question arises as to whether this motion can be made when your client informs you that he was not in possession of the contraband; that it was planted on him by the police. The answer is, quite obviously, yes; the officer will still have to testify as to how he seized the evidence and if his story itself describes an illegal search, then, without your client taking the stand, the motion to suppress should be granted. In this kind of fact pattern your client should not take the stand since his testimony will not allege an illegal search. Your moving papers in this type of case should simply say that your client was searched at a certain time and place (which will have happened in any event), that this search was illegal, and that he is now accused of possession of the contraband. Even where the officer's testimony describes a legal search or no search at all, his testimony can be rebutted by evidence other than the defendant's testimony which shows that his version of the facts is impossible, improbable, or contrary to human experience, and should not be believed.

The general rule is that searches and seizures are permissible only when they are incident to a lawful arrest, with a valid search warrant, or on consent. The law regarding search warrants will be covered in section C of this chapter. For searches incident to an arrest the key question becomes whether the facts as they appeared to the police officer gave him probable cause to arrest and whether the subsequent search exceeded the bounds of a search incident to the arrest. More frequently, the police allege that they observed contraband without a search and the arrest followed their observation of a crime. Your client may claim that he was simply stopped and searched, and the hearing on the motion to suppress involves a factual dispute as to what happened.

For cases in which there has been a valid arrest and a subsequent search turned up contraband or evidence of the crime, there is a body of cease law limiting searches incident to arrest. The most important case in this area is *Chimel vs. California*, 395 U.S. 752 (1969) in which the defendant was validly arrested in his home on a burglary charge and a search of his entire home followed. The Supreme Court held that only his person and the area into which the arrestee might reach in order to grab weapons or evidentiary items are all that can be searched without a warrant. This apparently means that not even the entire room where the arrest took place can be searched. Similarly, in *Shipley vs. California*, 395 U.S. 818 (1969), the Supreme Court held that where the defendant was arrested as he got out of his car, which was parked 15 to 20 feet from his house, a search of his home without a warrant was not lawful. In *Preston vs. California*, 376 U.S. 364 (1964), the defendants were arrested in a car for vagrancy, the car was towed away and impounded, and the court held that the subsequent search of the car was not incident to arrest and the evidence was inadmissible. In *Caver v. Kropp*, 306 F. Supp. 1329 (E.D. Mich. 1969), Caver was arrested on an attempted rape charge and three sealed envelopes found on him were opened and found to contain heroin. The court held that searches incident to arrests are limited to searches for weapons and proof of the crime for which the defendant was arrested, and therefore the opening of the envelopes without probable cause to believe that a crime had been committed was wrongful.

The rule that searches incident to lawful arrests can only be for weapons, instrumentalities, or fruits of the crime, is the law in New York since it has been enunciated by the Supreme Court and is based on the Fourth Amendment. For a discussion and cites to other cases, see *Warden v. Hayden*, 387 U.S. 294 (1967), and *Worthy v. U.S.*, 409 F.2d 1105 (1968). This does not mean, however, that if the search is permissible and other contraband is found that this other contraband is not admissible; it is. However, it does mean that the search must be limited by the reason for the arrest. For example, an arrest for drunken driving does not justify a search of the automobile, and an arrest for assault would appear to justify nothing more than a search of the person for weapons. A special problem arises in New York for arrests on minor charges such as violations where it is likely that the defendant would be released on a summons from the police station. In cases where the arrest is for disorderly conduct, harassment, or even loitering, it should be argued that the police have no authority to search any further than frisking the outside of the person's clothing for weapons. Your argument should be that since the search can only be for weapons (which can be accomplished by a frisk), or fruits of the crime (which do not exist in these cases), and since the defendant would be released on a summons (so no search can be made for the purpose of clearing defendant for incarceration), any search beyond a frisk is unlawful. There are many cases where arrests on very minor charges lead to discovery of drugs and the drugs would not have been found if the defendant had not been ordered to empty his pockets.

Section 140.50 of the Criminal Procedure Law contains New York's "stop and frisk" law. It states that "a police officer may stop a person in a public place . . . when he reasonably suspects that such person is committing, has committed, or is about to commit a felony or a Class A misdemeanor . . . and may demand of him his name, address and an explanation of his conduct." After such questioning, if the police officer reasonably suspects that he is in danger he may search such person for a dangerous weapon. The police have taken this section to mean that they can frisk almost anyone while in fact there has to be a basis for their suspecting the person whom they frisk. Their basis usually is either the conduct of the defendant or a report that they receive of a crime together with a description of the person who committed the crime. Often it can be shown that the circumstances or the report and description did not justify the police officer's suspicion against this particular defendant. More on this in the next section. Suffice it to say that searches made under this section should not go unchallenged. See *Terry v. Ohio*, 392 U.S. 1 (1967), and *Sibron v. New York*, 392 U.S. 40 (1967), for the Supreme Court's rulings on some of the limits of frisking and what can constitute probable cause to arrest. See also Justice Harlan's concurring opinion in *Sibron*, at page 74, in which he wrote: "If the nature of the suspected offense creates no reasonable apprehension for the officer's safety, I would not permit him to frisk unless other circumstances did so."

There is also a body of law holding that police misconduct, such as trespassing, even without a technical search, renders evidence found inadmissible. *People v. DeLeo*, 12 N.Y. 2d 913 (1963); *McDonald v. U.S.*, 335 U.S. 451 (1948). This situation could arise if there is a closed party and a police officer comes in plainclothes and says that he was invited by a friend of a friend and an arrest follows. Also, if a trespass by an undercover agent is the basis for a search warrant, in theory the warrant should be quashed.

Often the question arises as to whether the police must obtain a warrant before making a search, where they have probable cause and time to get a warrant, whether or not probable cause to make an arrest is present. For example, an ordinary citizen calls the police and tells them that a certain person has a pistol, and the police visit the apartment of that person and find a weapon. In this case they would have probable cause to get a warrant. The answer depends very much on the case but the Supreme Court has said that a warrant must be obtained whenever practicable. *Katz v. U.S.*, 389 U.S. 347 (1967); *Beck v. Ohio*, 379 U.S. 89 (1964); *Chapman v. U.S.*, 365 U.S. 610 (1961). The Supreme Court also said that in most instances failure to get a warrant can only be excused by emergency circumstances, such as where the police are actually pursuing a suspect. *Warden v. Hayden*, 387 U.S. 294 (1967).

Note that the Fourth Amendment to the Constitution also bars seizures without warrants unless they are incident to a lawful arrest. Thus there must be probable cause to believe that a crime has been committed before there can be a seizure. Where a police officer saw a man carrying a used portable television on the street during the day, and where there had not been any recent report of a stolen television of that description, and where the man was dressed in ordinary clothes and there was nothing otherwise suspicious about his behavior, the officer's seizure of the television was held to be improper, and the television was inadmissible even though it turned out later that the television was stolen. The defendant was able to give a reasonable account of his behavior (he said that he had purchased the TV from a friend whom he named and that he was taking the TV home). (Case unreported.) However, the stop and frisk law may authorize the initial questioning, and, if the defendant's answers had been inconsistent or the defendant's behavior suspicious at the time of questioning, then there might have been probable cause to arrest and seize.

The standard story heard throughout the Criminal Court since *Mapp v. Ohio*, 367 U.S. 643 (1961), is called the "dropsey" story. In it the officer testifies that as he approached the defendant, the defendant dropped to the ground glassine envelopes (or marijuana cigarettes or hypodermic needles, as the case may be), the officer picked it up, examined it, found that it appeared to be contraband, and placed the defendant under arrest. The standard story you will hear from your client is that the police walked up to him and simply searched him either in the street, or, more commonly, in a hallway.

It is my opinion that virtually everyone in the courthouse

knows that most dropsey stories are fabrications but the judges accept the police officer's testimony because they believe the defendant to be actually guilty of the crime and they do not want him to escape on a technicality. Also, many judges do not wish to offend the police and prosecutors by upsetting a process that has become systematized. See Judge Irving Younger's opinion in *People v. McNulty*, New York Law Journal, 9/18/70, p. 19 (Crim. Ct., New York Co.), in which he frankly stated that the frequency of the dropsey stories, and the fact that there was a marked increase in their number after *Mapp*, indicated their suspiciousness. However, he denied the motion to suppress in the case and said that only the prosecutor could solve the problem. Nevertheless, dropsey stories can occasionally be beaten. Surprisingly, several jury trials have resulted in acquittals where the officer used the dropsey story and the defendant did not take the stand. The problem is that the motion to suppress is decided by the judge prior to trial and the only issue before the jury is whether the defendant possessed the contraband, not whether there was an improper search. Nevertheless, now that jury trials are available it is possible to go to trial in a dropsey case even after losing a motion to suppress. The theory of the case can be that the officer is lying, his story is on its face inconsistent with ordinary human behavior and therefore there is a reasonable doubt about guilt.

In dropsey cases all the standard means of showing that the police officer is lying should be employed. Other officers present at the time of arrest should be subpoenaed, his testimony should be compared with what he said at the preliminary hearing, the cross-examination should be close enough to try to bring out inconsistencies and impossibilities, and other witnesses and the defendant should take the stand. Where the defendant has a long record, it can often be helpful for him to simply state that when he has contraband on his person he would never be stupid enough to throw it to the ground in front of a police officer; his experience in being arrested has taught him that such an act would be lunacy. Of course, independent witnesses who were not arrested are invaluable. If the defendant was actually in possession of the contraband, he should openly admit it at the hearing on the motion to suppress; it forms the basis for the motion since he is alleging an illegal search, it makes his testimony more credible, and his admissions are not admissible at trial. *Simmons v. U.S.*, 390 U.S. 377 (1968). But see *Peo. v. Harris*, 28 L. Ed. 2d 1 (1971), p. 81. If you are very ambitious you might even try to find out how often the officer has used the dropsey story in the past, perhaps by asking him or subpoenaing his memo book and checking on the arrests he made.

Another method of beating a dropsey story is to show that the evidence that was dropped was not abandoned and did not appear on its face to be contraband. Frequently, contraband such as glassine envelopes or hypodermic needles are wrapped either in envelopes, eyeglass cases, or cigarette packs, and the officer testifies that the package was dropped and that he opened it, found it to be contraband, and thereupon arrested the defendant. Most police officers do not know that the evidence must appear to be abandoned before it can be searched and in their zeal to get an airtight case, they testify that the evidence was dropped by the defendant near his foot, that they never lost sight of it, and that they immediately picked it up and searched it. In *People v. Anderson*, 24 N.Y. 2d 12, 298 NYS 2d 698 (1969), the defendant dropped a tin box on to the street out of a parked car and the court held that these facts did not on their face show an abandonment.

Where the police officer's testimony clearly indicates an abandonment the defendant should not take the stand, since, if he does, and his story is diametrically opposed to that of the police officer, some judges have held simply that they found the defendant's testimony unbelievable and therefore they denied the motion to suppress. Once a lack of abandonment has been shown, stop your questioning; do not give the officer a chance to embellish his story with other circumstances that could justify a search.

Another common story told by police officers is that the evidence was in plain view and the police officers saw it when they were going about some lawful business. For example, the police came to an apartment to tell the tenants to turn down their phonograph and when the tenants opened the door they saw marijuana cigarettes on the table; when the police stopped a car and asked for the license and registration in a routine check, they saw what appeared to be a gun barrel sticking out from under the seat; or simply that they saw one defendant hand to another a glassine envelope. Again the standard methods of discrediting police testimony, set forth above, must be employed. In addition, however, an effort should be made to recreate the factual situation, either through investigators visiting the scene, diagrams, or reenactment in the courtroom, in order to show that the testimony of the police was impossible. In the apartment situation for example, pictures, diagrams of layouts, and the testimony of an investigator as to what is visible from the door are important. Where the facts warrant you should even request that the court make an on-site inspection. If your motion for an on-site inspection is granted, it means that court is reconvened, with judge, bailiff, court reporter, District Attorney, defense attorney, and defendant, at the scene of the alleged illegal search. Remember that policemen are accustomed to virtually no challenges to their testimony other than an occasional defendant taking the stand, and if you do not appear to be overly aggressive at the preliminary hearing, you can lull them into a false sense of security so that their testimony may be sloppy.

In the automobile situation you should again try to recreate the circumstances by finding out the time, the exact location in relation to traffic lights and overhead lights, the type of car, and the exact place in the car where the officer allegedly saw the contraband. Defense counsel or an investigator can try to duplicate the circumstances to ascertain if it was possible for the officer to see inside the car. Important questions to be asked at the preliminary hearings are exactly where the officer was standing, whether he had a flash light, what else he saw in the car, and exactly what he saw that appeared to be contraband. Depending on the circumstances, your object should be to show that he could not have seen what he says he saw, or that even if he did, the items would have appeared to him to be non-contraband.

In a simple case where the officer says he saw a glassine envelope pass from one defendant to another, the exact locations of all persons are crucial so that distances can be measured. Once the distance is ascertained, the alleged observations can be duplicated in the courtroom. For example, if the officer saw the contraband across the street from a distance of 40 feet, you could place a piece of paper in one hand and a glassine envelope in the other, stand 40 feet away, and ask the officer to identify each.

Another commonly alleged basis for a search is that the police had a report of a crime and a description of the suspect that resembled the defendant. If the report and the description actually gave the police reasonable ground to believe that the defendant has committed the crime, then the arrest and subsequent search would be proper. However, if the defendant is not actually the suspect, then it can often be shown that the facts were such that the police should have known that the defendant was not their man. In this kind of case you must subpoena the police department records of communications made relating to the crime for which the defendant was initially stopped. The hearing should then be a detailed analysis of the description of the suspect, the actual description of the defendant, the time and place of the crime, the actual time and place that the defendant was stopped, the direction that the alleged assailant was thought to have taken when he fled, the direction that the defendant was traveling, whether it was possible to reach the location where the defendant was stopped within the time interval between the commission of the crime and the time the defendant was stopped, whether the defendant was traveling toward the area where the crime was committed, and whether the defendant's behavior was suspicious in any other way. By bringing out all these details it can often be shown that the police officer should have known that the defendant was not their man.

Consent is another basis for legitimizing an otherwise illegal search. Consent must be knowingly and freely given in order to be valid. Where consent is alleged, the state has the burden of proving that the consent was voluntary, and it depends on the totality of the circumstances. *People vs. Whitehurst*, 25 N.Y. 2d 389, 306 NYS 2d 673 (1970); *Bumper v. North Carolina*, 391 U.S. 543 (1968). When the police began to question in an accusatory manner, or where the questioning takes place under circumstances that indicate that the defendant is effectively restrained, even though nothing has been said, the consent should be found to have been involuntarily given. *People vs. Whitehurst, supra.*

The consent can also be limited. When the police officer asks "mind if we come in and look around?" this is not a consent to tear the house apart as is usually done in searches. In *Judd vs. United States*, 89 U.S. App. D.C. 64, 190 F.2d 649 (1951), the court held that the defendant, while under arrest, did not give actual consent to the police to search his apartment even though he said they could go into the apartment. The court intimated that consent given while under arrest is almost always invalid.

The time of arrest, or effective restraint, is important in cases where consent to a search is in issue. In *Kelly vs. United States*, 111 U.S. App. D.C. 396, 298 F.2d 310 (1961), the defendant was sitting in a restaurant, two police officers asked him to step outside, one led the way while the other followed either behind or next to him, and, when asked what he had in his pockets, he admitted that he had marijuana. The court held that under these circumstances there was no consent. It should be argued that any consent given while under effective restraint is invalid. Where consent is in issue your questioning should bring out the exact conversation, as close to verbatim as possible, that took place between the police and defendant, where the conversation took place, the time of day, defendant's condition (was he drunk or injured), how many police officers were present, whether any threats or promises were made, and who started the conversation. You should also simply ask the officer if the defendant was free to go at any point during the conversation. Needless to say, you should not be surprised if you find the police lying in situations like this.

At the close of a motion to suppress, particularly a complicated one, you should deliver a summation. You should briefly summarize the testimony given, give your evaluation of its credibility, point out inconsistencies and impossibilities, stress the fact that police lying in this area is notorious and that the police have a stake in lying since they want convictions, and stress the credibility of independent witnesses if there are any. Where there are questions of law you can deliver an oral argument on the law, citing cases, and you can offer to the court that you are prepared to submit a brief if the court will reserve decision in the case.

C. Motions to Controvert Search Warrants

In a small percentage of cases search warrants will have been obtained by the arresting officer and the arrest will follow the authorized search. However, the police find it cumbersome to obtain warrants, and, since the warrants are often successfully controverted, most policemen prefer the time honored method of alleging that the goods were in plain view. Wherever a search warrant has been obtained, you should, following the preliminary hearing, make a motion on papers to controvert (or quash) the warrant and suppress the evidence on the ground that it was illegally obtained.

In order to obtain a search warrant the police officer goes to the District Attorney's office and, using the information supplied by the officer, a petition for a search warrant, an affidavit in support of the petition, and the search warrant itself are prepared. These papers are then submitted to a justice of the Supreme Court, ex parte of course, and, after what is usually a cursory examination, the judge signs the warrant. The affidavit, of course, must show probable cause. Warrants are also signed by the Criminal Court judge sitting in the arraignment part. You must obtain a copy of these papers yourself, either from the District Attorney's office, or, depending on which court issued the warrant, the Supreme Court Clerk's office or the clerk's office of the arraignment part. The papers are filed under the address of the premises searched, not by the name of the defendant.

Hearings on motions to controvert must be thoroughly prepared for. The warrant and affidavit in support must be obtained, very carefully read, and researched if necessary. Very few judges know the law in this area well and citations and photocopies of cases can be crucial. Unless the papers are defective on their face, however, you will not be able to brief the issues fully until after the hearing when all the facts are in. A convenient practice is to ask for an adjournment after the hearing for the purpose of submitting a brief. As with any other motion, you are required to serve motion papers five days prior to the adjourned date. See appendix, page 142.

The question of whether the affidavit has shown probable cause to the judge who signed the warrant, and the question of whether all the procedural requirements have been complied with, are reviewable de novo at the hearing on the motion to controvert the search warrant and suppress the evidence. Also reviewable are whether the statements contained in the affidavit are true. *People v. Alfinito*, 16 N.Y. 2d 181, 264 N.Y.S. 2d 243 (1965).

The hearing should begin with the introduction into evidence of the warrant and affidavit. This is done by showing the papers to the arresting officer while he is on the stand, asking him to identify them as the papers he submitted to court and later used to conduct the search that resulted in this arrest, and then offering them into evidence as defendant's exhibits 1 and 2. You will probably have photocopies of the originals which are theoretically not admissible but the D.A. will almost invariably stipulate to the fact that the copies are the same as the originals, to avoid the delay of having to subpoena the originals from the Clerk's office.

Your cross-examination and preparation should begin with questions on whether all the procedural requirements for obtaining and executing a search warrant have been met. Here are some of the requirements.

1. Where the affidavit is not sufficient on its face, and the judge questions the police officer to elicit more information, this must be under oath and transcribed or summarized, or the search warrant is void. *People v. Asaro*, 57 Misc. 2d 373, 291 N.Y.S. 2d 613 (1968).

2. Section 690.35 of the Criminal Procedure Law provides that doors or windows cannot be broken into by a police officer, unless (a) after announcing himself and stating that he has a search warrant, he is refused admission, or (b) the judge has inserted an order permitting the breaking in without warning, but this order may not be inserted unless proof is given to the judge that the contraband may be quickly disposed of, or that giving warning will endanger the officer. The proof that is required for a no-knock order must be specific facts (which can be hearsay) but cannot consist only of conclusory statements. This proof must be contained in the affidavit and cannot be added to by testimony given at the hearing on the motion to controvert. If the affidavit contained no proof, but only conclusory statements, you should not elicit more facts; simply read the affidavit into the record and argue for suppression at the end of the hearing. If the affidavit does contain some proof, make the officer spell out in detail exactly how he came by this

proof, what was said to him, by whom, when, how reliable is his informant, what proof of reliability does he have, etc. (see p. 76).

3. Section 690.35 of the Criminal Procedure Law provides that the warrant can be executed only between 6:00 A.M. and 9:00 P.M. unless the judge inserts an order that the warrant can be executed at night, which he may do only if there is a showing that the warrant cannot be executed during the day or that the goods will be removed forthwith unless seized immediately. The section is similar in nature to section 690.35 discussed above in paragraph 2. It is not clear whether a warrant with an invalid section 690.35 order in it must be quashed if the warrant was executed during the day without resort to breaking in. You should argue that in general warrants are strictly construed and that where the warrant is partially not supported by probable cause, it should be totally void.

4. If the warrant is not executed within 10 days of its issuance it is absolutely void. Section 690.30 of the Criminal Procedure Law. The arresting officer is also required to forthwith make a "return," which means he is required to bring the evidence seized and an affidavit of what was seized to the issuing judge, but failure to promptly file a return will not by itself be grounds for quashing the warrant.

5. The warrant must be executed properly. Unless a 690.35 order is inserted, it must be shown to the defendant before the search, and only those items described can be seized unless other contraband is found. Where a warrant listed nine titles of obscene books and only one-fifth of the books seized came from the nine titles, the entire search was held to be void. *People v. Bosco*, 56 Misc. 2d 1080, 290 N.Y.S. 2d 481 (1968). You can cite this case to show that the state is held to a strict standard of conduct in the execution of search warrants.

The place to be searched and the property to be seized must be particularly described, although the defendant need not be named. General searches are prohibited. Failure of the papers to meet these requirements, even if the search is later properly limited, makes the search warrant void. See *People v. Rothenberg*, 20 N.Y. 2d 35, 281 N.Y.S. 2d 316 (1967), where a search warrant authorizing seizure of "obscene, indecent and hard core pornography" was held void for failure to particularly describe items to be seized, since it delegated to the police officer the function of determining what is obscene. A search warrant describing "furniture and household goods" was held void for failure to specify which goods belonged to the company who had lost them. *People v. Coletti*, 39 Misc. 2d 580, 241 N.Y.S. 2d 454 (1953).

Similarly, where the place to be searched is not accurately designated, the warrant is void. Where the warrant described a building containing two apartments and defendant lived only in one of them, the search warrant was held to be void. *People v. Rainey*, 14 N.Y. 2d 35, 248 N.Y.S. 2d 33 (1964). Watch for mistakes in apartment numbers and locations of apartments; a mistake makes the warrant and search void, and in tenements the locations and numbers of apartments can be confusing.

Frequently search warrants are based on tips from informers. The rule in these cases is that the issuing magistrate must be informed (1) of some of the underlying circumstances upon which the informer based his statements, and (2) the basis for the officer's belief that the informer is reliable. *People v. Montague*, 19 N.Y. 2d 121, 278 N.Y.S. 2d 372 (1967). *Aguilar v. Texas*, 378 U.S. 108 (1964). Hearsay is of course admissible as a basis for either requirement. *People v. Rodgers*, 15 N.Y. 2d 422, 260 N.Y.S. 2d 433 (1965).

Not infrequently affidavits fail to set forth in detail the basis for the informer's statements. Whether the affidavit is sufficient depends on the particular case. Again an insufficient affidavit cannot be cured by the police officer or even the informer filling holes at the hearing on the motion to suppress. Your efforts should be directed toward showing that the basis for the informer's statements was indefinite, ambiguous, and conclusory. For example, where the informer said that he saw known drug addicts going in and out of a tenement apartment occupied by the defendant, you should ask whether the informer related the names of everyone living in the apartment (which might be exculpatory to your client if there were others), where he was standing when he saw the visitors come and go, the names of the alleged addicts, how he knows that they are addicts, the times of the visits, how long each visitor stayed, exactly how many people came during specific intervals of time, whether the visitors came singly or in groups, whether any of the visitors had friends or relatives in other apartments, etc. The technique is to set up straw men to show the inadequacy of the information and to show that the information could have had an innocent meaning. This line of questioning is designed to show that the informer did not tell the officer enough about the basis for his information (or give enough information), and the police officer in turn did not relate enough facts to the judge, and therefore the affidavit itself does not contain sufficient information to give the issuing judge probable cause to sign the warrant.

Reliability of informants is generally shown by a statement in the affidavit by the officer that the informer has furnished information in the past which led to a certain number of convictions. The statement in the affidavit need not name specific cases, but on cross you can ask for cases and dates of arrest, and then you can request a 30-minute recess during which time you can check the papers on these cases to see if there were convictions. You can also ask for all the cases in which the informer proved unreliable. The answer could show only a one out of two success rate, which would make him unreliable.

Most courts are of the opinion that the informer need never be disclosed. This is not correct. The Supreme Court, in *McCray v. Illinois*, 386 U.S. 300 (1967) held that the identity need not be divulged where "the arresting officers . . . testified . . . fully and in precise detail as to what the informer told them and as to why they had reason to believe his information." 386 U.S. at 313. If the officer is vague and evasive in testifying about what the informant said, you should cite *McCray* and demand that the informant be produced. You should argue that the officer's testimony indicates that the informant does not even exist. The judge of course will not want the informant to be uncovered and you may be able to compromise by having the informant appear in secret in the judge's chambers. An order for the informant to appear, even in secrecy, can result in the case being dismissed simply because the informant will not come and the police will not force him to come because they do not want to lose him.

The informant must also be disclosed when his testimony

might be helpful to a defense on the merits. *Roviaro v. U.S.*, 353 U.S. 53 (1957). There are many cases in which you can claim that the informer's testimony would be exculpatory. If the informer alleged that drugs were being sold from a particular apartment and you can state that more than one person lives there, then the informer's testimony could clear one or more of the residents.

Your questioning should also seek to discredit the informer by inquiring into his occupation, his life style, whether he has a criminal record, whether he is or was a drug addict, and what his incentive is to be an informer. Many informers are themselves addicts with cases pending (particularly federal cases) and they receive promises of suspended sentences for information. If this is the case, you should argue that such an informer is never considered reliable as a defendant since his incentive to lie is his freedom, and thus he should not be considered to be reliable as an informer since his incentive to furnish any kind of information is also his freedom.

Section 690.40 of the CPL gives the judge the power to order witnesses to appear before him and testify. It is this section that authorizes the judge to direct that the informant appear. Defense counsel of course can subpoena the police officer's partner, if he has one, to try to bring out inconsistencies.

Last but not least, the affidavit in support of the search warrant must itself show probable cause to believe that a crime has been or is being committed and that a search of a particular premises will reveal evidence of that crime. Whether this requirement is met depends on the facts of each case. Known bookmakers entering on various occasions a private dwelling with two unlisted phones has been held not to show probable cause. *People v. Fino*, 14 N.Y. 2d 160, 250 N.Y.S. 2d 47 (1964). Where the driver of a car was arrested for drunken driving, there is no probable cause for a warrant to search his car. *People v. Beaman*, 44 Misc. 2d 336, 253 N.Y.S. 2d 674 (1964). Observations of known addicts repeatedly entering a multiple dwelling was held not to give probable cause to search a particular apartment in the building (case unreported).

D. Motions to Suppress Statements and Confessions

Hearings on motions to suppress statements or confessions

are commonly called *Huntley* hearings after *People v. Huntley*, 15 N.Y. 2d (1965), which required that such hearings be held prior to trial. Whenever the government intends to introduce into evidence any statements made by the defendant, Section 710.30 of the Criminal Procedure Law requires that the government give notice of its intent to introduce such statements prior to trial. Such notices (formerly called "813(F) notices" after the old Code) are often given in the form of a little slip of paper at the arraignment. Since you may not have represented the defendant at the arraignment, you may not be aware of the fact that a notice has been served. Whenever a notice is served that fact is noted by the judge on the court papers and for this reason, as well as to find out the past history of the case, you should always closely examine the court papers as soon as you enter a case. Whenever a notice has been served, you should make a motion on papers to suppress the statement or confession, if for no other reason than to find out exactly what statements the defendant is alleged to have made.

Hearings on motions to suppress confessions, probably more than any other, often boil down to a swearing contest between the defendant and the police on what actually happened and what actually was said. The problems of proof are enormous. The only other witnesses to the questioning are other police officers and perhaps other persons arrested that day who were waiting in the precinct house for transfer to court. Where the issue is whether the defendant was advised of his rights, other police officers may or may not be helpful; they may simply bolster each other's testimony. However, where the defendant's responses to the warnings could indicate absence of a waiver of constitutional rights, or where the length of time of defendant's interrogation is in issue, other officers who participated or sat in on the interrogation should definitely be subpoenaed. The names of other persons arrested who may have overheard the manner of questioning or who may have seen whether the defendant was mistreated and how long he was questioned, can be gotten from a log book in the precinct house.

There are two basic issues at *Huntley* hearings: whether the confession was voluntary under cases preceding *Miranda v. Arizona*, 384 U.S. 436 (1966), and whether the *Miranda* warnings were given and the defendant knowingly, intelligently, and voluntarily waived his constitutional rights. On the question of voluntariness of a confession, the court looks to the totality of the circumstances and decides on a case by case basis. Prior to *Miranda* a substantial body of law was formed regarding voluntariness. Physical or mental infirmaties that reduce the will to resist can be a basis for finding that a confession was involuntary. *Blackburn v. Alabama*, 361 U.S. 199 (1960); *Culombe v. Connecticut*, 367 U.S. 568 (1961). You will have the burden of going forward with evidence of infirmities and of their effect on the defendant's will to resist, by medical and psychiatric testimony. You should also prepare a memorandum of law in this kind of case.

Police brutality or threats of brutality will of course make a confession involuntary, but such conduct in pursuance of a confession is no longer commonplace. The problem of proof in these circumstances is enormous. Evidence of defendant's physical condition after arrest can be gotten either from hospital records, observations of a lawyer, or photographs if someone has the foresight to take them if and when the defendant is bailed out. Where there are beatings (and this applies also to demonstration arrests) the police usually charge the defendants with assault or resisting arrest, and the police claim injuries themselves. The officers often go to the hospital for "treatment" of their "injury," which is often no more than a black and blue mark. If the officer testifies at the preliminary hearing that he did go to the hospital, you should subpoena the hospital records and try to ascertain from the police and hospital records the time when the officer left the precinct. It may be many hours after the arrest, which indicates that the injury probably did not warrant treatment, if it existed at all. The injury may be such that it could not have been gotten from an assault by the defendant, such as an injury to the hand. I once heard a police officer testify to being struck in the hand; an attempted reenactment of this scene revealed its impossibility.

Frightening, undressing, denying food or drugs, promising leniency, or using a friend or relative, or psychological trick (such as telling the defendant that his partner confessed and implicated him), can also invalidate a confession. In heavy cases the questioning may be prolonged, and in homicide cases a District Attorney is usually brought in to assist in questioning. The long interrogation, particularly if combined with other facts such as a poor psychological state and a low will to resist, can itself make a confession involuntary. For cases on this subject and more detail on the law, see *Law and Tactics in Exclusionary Hearings*, Chapter 8. In cases where you are alleging any of these circumstances you should prepare a memorandum of law since the courts are not familiar with the various fact patterns that have made confessions inadmissible. Again, proof is the most difficult problem and even with witnesses and corroborating evidence you will have a hard time getting a court to rule that there has been police misconduct or that a confession is involuntary.

The Supreme Court's decision in *Miranda v. Arizona, supra*, has substantially altered the law in this area. Its holding in essence is that any statements or confessions made while the defendant is in custody (as opposed to arrest) are inadmissible unless the defendant has been given certain particularly prescribed warnings of his constitutional rights and he has knowingly, voluntarily and intelligently waived those rights.

The first question is whether the defendant was actually or effectively in custody at the time the statements were made. Pre-custody statements are admissible without *Miranda* warnings. The lines between custodial and investigatory interrogation are not clear but it is clear that custody can occur long before formal arrest. Custodial interrogation means that the questions are more than investigatory, that the defendant is the focus of the investigation, and that the defendant was effectively not free to go even though an arrest had not been made. In cross-examining on this issue you should bring out exactly what information the police had prior to questioning, how they got it, how directly it pointed to defendant, whether anyone else was being questioned, where the questioning took place, the manner and circumstance of the questioning, how many police officers were present, etc., and you should directly ask the police officer whether the defendant was free to leave before or during the questioning. In one case a boy's mother called the police to report that she found marijuana in her son's coat. The police came to the apartment, took the marijuana out of the coat, and asked the defendant if the coat was his. His admission that the coat belonged to him was held to be inadmissible. (Case unreported.)

Where the questioning begins in a clearly investigatory stage but the answers to the questions start to become suspicious, it should be argued that as soon as the officer became suspicious, the *Miranda* warnings should have been given, and any statements made subsequent to the first suspicious answer should be inadmissible. The theory for this is that as soon as the officer became suspicious the defendant effectively became in custody and the defendant became the focus of the investigation.

The *Miranda* warnings are:

1. The individual "must be informed in clear and unequivocal terms that he has the right to remain silent."
2. He must be warned that "anything said can and will be used against the individual in court."
3. He must be informed that "he has the right to consult with a lawyer and to have a lawyer with him during interrogation."
4. He must be informed that "if he is indigent a lawyer will be appointed to represent him."

If any of the above warnings are omitted, any statements obtained from an individual become inadmissible. However, note that *Peo. v. Harris*, 28 L. Ed. 1 (1971) permits an otherwise inadmissible statement to be used to impeach testimony at trial.

Where the officer testifies simply that he gave the defendant the required warnings, you should ask him on cross exactly what he said to the defendant. The police department has distributed cards to all officers which contain the *Miranda* warnings and the police officer will often testify that he read the contents of the card to the defendant. In such cases you should ask the officer to read the card in court as he did to the defendant. The warnings must be clearly and understandably given; if they are not, *Miranda* has been violated. If the officer has read them very quickly to the defendant, he may duplicate his manner of delivery in court.

The Supreme Court in *Miranda* placed a "heavy burden" on the government of showing that there has been a knowing, intelligent, and voluntary waiver of constitutional rights. Your cross-examination should therefore bring out any responses the defendant made to the warnings. If the defendant indicated at any time that he did not wish to make a statement or that he wanted a lawyer, the questioning must stop. If the interrogation continues and the defendant later makes a statement, the statement is inadmissible. Generally the police officer will testify that the defendant was silent or that he answered "yes" when asked if he understood the warnings, and that, at some point thereafter he made a statement. If the testimony indicates that the interrogation continued for a substantial period of time, or even for half an hour or an hour, before the defendant made a statement, it should be argued that the defendant's silence at the beginning of the interrogation indicated that he did not wish to make a statement and the questioning should have stopped then. It can also be argued that the defendant was pressured into waiving his rights; that a statement made after lengthy interrogation, long after the warnings were given, cannot indicate a free and voluntary waiver of constitutional rights, especially where the government has a heavy burden of showing voluntariness.

E. Motions to Suppress Identifications
(Wade Hearings)

When a suspect is identified by the victim of a crime at a lineup or showup the circumstances of the identification can be prejudicial to the defendant or they can be violative of the defendant's right to counsel. If improper, the evidence of the particular improper identification may be inadmissible in evidence at trial, and, depending on the circumstances, the bad identification can taint all later identifications, including an in-court identification, and the state will then have to rely on other evidence to prove its case. It is clear that for many kinds of cases, particularly robberies, winning a motion to suppress a particular identification and all subsequent identifications can be dispositive of the case. A *Wade* Hearing, as such motions to suppress are called, can also be an invaluable pre-trial discovery device in which you will hear the entire testimony of the complainant as well as his testimonial ability.

There are two types of identifications: lineups and showups. In a lineup a witness views a group of people and is asked to pick out the one whom he thinks is guilty of the crime, while in a showup the victim views the suspect alone and is asked if he is the guilty party.

The law in this area is recent, confusing and not fully developed. The three principal cases in this area are *U.S. v. Wade*, 388 U.S. 218 (1967), *Gilbert v. California*, 388 U.S. 263 (1967), and *Stovall v. Denno*, 388 U.S. 293 (1967). To briefly summarize, *Wade* and *Gilbert* held that the defendant had the right to have counsel present at a pre-trial post-indictment line-up and that if counsel were not present or waived, the evidence of the identification is inadmissible in evidence, and any subsequent in-court identification is inadmissible unless the state can show clear and convincing evidence that the in-court identification had a basis independent of the improper identification. *Stovall* held that *Wade* and *Gilbert* were to be prospectively applied but the court also said that confrontations could be so suggestive that they violate due process and become inadmissible in evidence, the vague test being, the "totality of the circumstances." 388 U.S. at 302. Thus there are two grounds for excluding an identification: lack of counsel and where the procedure of the identification violated due process.

The time at which an accused gains a right to counsel at a confrontation is not clear (*Wade* and *Gilbert* deal only with post-indictment identifications). It should be argued that the right to counsel attaches as soon as there is a showup or lineup since these are crucial stages of the proceedings, the results of which can severely prejudice the defendant. The state will counter by claiming unfeasibility of providing counsel and undue hampering of law enforcement efforts, and in the end the courts will probably hold that an accused has a right to counsel only where it is feasible without unduly hampering law enforcement efforts. The circumstances regarding the feasibility of having a lineup with a lawyer present are therefore important. See *Commonwealth v. Bumpus*, 354 Mass. 494, 238 N.E. 2d 343 (1968), and *U.S. v. Davis*, 399 F. 2d 948 (2d Cir. 1968), discussed below.

The question of whether a lineup is so suggestive of the defendant as to violate due process depends upon the totality of the circumstances and common sense should tell you what factors are important. The complainant and police officers should be questioned in detail on factors such as how closely the persons in the lineup fit the general description of the accused, was the defendant the only one who looked seedy or clean cut, and did the defendant look special or was he treated differently from the others in any way, such as by being escorted by policemen. If you are present at a lineup you should take notes of all these factors and take down the names and addresses of persons in the lineup for possible re-enactment in court.

Showups on the other hand are by their very nature suggestive. Only the accused is presented to the witness and the fact that the accused is in the custody of the police is itself suggestive. However, even a showup can be made more or less suggestive by the manner in which the accused is treated, whether he is gruffly ordered or pushed around, whether he is handcuffed, and what is said to the witness about the circumstances under which he was picked up.

The admissibility of a showup identification has not yet been decisively ruled upon by the Supreme Court. At the present time the criteria the courts employ are (1) the probable accuracy of the showup identification, considering the opportunity the witness had to observe the defendant at the time of the crime and (2) the feasibility of conducting a lineup. See *U.S. ex rel Rutherford v. Deegan*, 406 F. 2d 217 (2d Cir. 1969), *Simmons v. U.S.*, 391 U.S. (1968), and *Biggers v. Tennessee*, 391 U.S. 404 (1968). It has been suggested in an excellent law note on this subject in the *N.Y.U. Law Review* (44 N.Y.U.L. Rev. 377 [1969]) that the law in this area may become that showup identifications are per se violative of due process and inadmissible wherever a lineup is feasible and you should so argue at *Wade* Hearings, for a possible appealable issue. At present the feasibility of a lineup seems to be only a factor to be considered in deciding whether a particular showup violates due process, *Wright v. U.S.*, 404 F. 2d 1256 (D.C. Cir. 1968).

Two cases in which courts have admitted showup identifications are *Commonwealth v. Bumpus, supra,* and *U.S. v. Davis, supra.* In *Bumpus* the accused was picked up shortly after a burglary and identified at the witness' home. The court admitted the identification on the ground that requiring a lineup would unduly hamper law enforcement efforts since, if Bumpus were the wrong man, the delay might permit the guilty party to escape. In *Davis* the defendant, walking on the Thruway near a car, was picked up for the traffic infraction of walking on the Thruway, and identified by the toll collector as the driver of a stolen car before anyone knew that it was stolen. The important factors here were that the circumstance of the defendant being in custody were not suggestive since no one knew that a crime had been committed, and also that a lineup was obviously impractical.

Typical fact patterns of identifications after arrest are (1) the defendant is arrested within minutes or hours after the commission of a crime, such as a robbery or burglary, and the arrest is based on his description and attire; and (2) the arrest follows the crime by several days or weeks and is based on a description and perhaps also a name or nickname. Delayed arrests are frequently for crimes such as selling drugs to an undercover agent, statutory rape, or crimes of violence where the complainant knows the defendant, although they can also be for robberies or burglaries. When the arrest is within hours of the crime, some relevant factors on the feasibility of a lineup would be (1) whether there is a pressing need for an immediate confrontation, such as when the complainant may be dying; (2) the time it would take to set up a lineup and whether the delay would unduly hamper law enforcement (i.e., if the defendant was picked up by chance several hours after the crime because he fit the description of the assailant, and if the search for persons of his description was continuing despite the fact that the defendant was in custody, then a slight delay to set up a lineup would not unduly hamper the police); and (3) the time intervals and circumstances between the crime, arrest and identification, e.g., if the arrest follows within minutes of the crime and the identification is made moments later at the scene of the crime, a lineup seems unfeasible, while if the arrest is made in the middle of the night an hour or two after the crime, and the witness was awakened to come down to the police station, then it should be argued that a lineup was feasible if the confrontation would have been delayed until morning. When the arrest follows the crime by days or weeks, and it would take several hours or even as much as a day to set up a lineup, it should be argued that the relative delay is unimportant, a lineup is always feasible, and the showup identification is per se violative of due process and therefore inadmissible.

Once an identification has been suppressed, either because of lack of counsel or due to a violation of due process, the question becomes whether the bad identification has tainted all later identifications, including an in-court identification. The later identifications will not be permitted, and the state will have to rely on other evidence, unless the state can show that the later identifications have a source other than the suppressed identification. In deciding this the court looks to (1) the opportunity the witness had to observe the defendant at the time of the crime; if the witness got a good long look, then the in-court identification would be allowed; and (2) the existence of any discrepancy (or lack of discrepancy) between any pre-arrest description and the defendant's actual description. If the in-court identification is not allowed, the case is almost certain to be dismissed, unless the state can identify the defendant as the culprit by some other means.

Whether or not the showup identification is suppressed, if you suspect that the witness will have difficulty picking the defendant out of a lineup prior to trial, you should make a motion that a lineup be conducted, or you can set one up in court yourself. If the *Wade* Hearing is held before such a lineup can take place, you can have the defendant appear in court hooded to avoid spoiling the lineup.

The new C.P.L., § 710.30, requires that the state give notice to the defendant whenever it intends to introduce evidence of an identification. This notice will be similar to the notice of intent to introduce statements; the D.A. will state at some early stage of the proceeding that identification evidence will be introduced, the D.A. will hand a slip of paper to defense counsel, and the judge will note on the papers that notice has been given.

Chapter 8

YOUTHS

All cases in which one or more of the defendants is between the ages of 16 and 19 years (under 19 at the time the crime was committed), are handled in Part 3 of the Criminal Court, the youth part. Where there are co-defendants who are over 19, their cases are handled in Part 3 also. This includes both felonies and misdemeanors.

When the charges are felonies, the procedures outlined in Chapter 4B on adult felony cases apply to youths also. The court has jurisdiction only to set bail, hold preliminary hearings, or reduce the case to a misdemeanor. The difference between part 3 and others is that cases are much more readily reduced to misdemeanors when the defendant is young. Felonious assault, burglary, purse snatching where no one was hurt, and drug cases are frequently reduced to misdemeanors for youths, especially for a plea, where for adults the same cases might be sent to the grand jury for indictment.

Another key difference between youths and adults is that the court will be more lenient, when considering parole or a reduction in bail, or in sentencing, if parents, relatives, social workers, psychologists, counselor, or clergymen are present. Most judges will also more readily parole a defendant into a drug program when the defendant is young, as described in Chapter 4E. When making a bail application or at the time of sentencing, such persons should personally appear in court or, if that is too impractical, letters from agencies or individuals can be given to the judge.

When handling cases against youths you should keep in mind that the legal aspects are often less important than the personal social and psychological problems of the defendant. At your first interview with him, you should inquire as to what the defendant is doing with his life, whether he is in school, whether he is working, when he has last worked, how long he held his previous job, whether he has a heroin or cocaine problem, how bad his drug problem is, and generally whether he has any hopes or plans for the immediate or distant future. The reason for this is that you may be the only person who can push him or guide him into seeking help for his problems. Of course, as a lawyer, you may not be able to make valid decisions as to what should be done, but you can seek the assistance of a social worker or other competent persons and refer the defendant to those people. In addition to wanting to help him for his own sake, you should keep in mind that even for relatively serious crimes, the court will grant probation to youngsters who appear to be doing something constructive with their lives.

Many judges, even the more conservative ones, agree that jail is at best a waste of time for youths, and even in serious cases they will go along with any alternative that offers the defendant treatment or keeps him off the streets. Among some of the things available to youths who are facing jail are private homes, usually funded by religious institutions; job corps; New York State Division for Youth camps; and even state training schools (reformatories) which are actually only for youths under 16, but youths over 16 who have just been released can be re-admitted. Many people will say that these alternatives are not good ones, but most will agree that they are better than the Rikers Island Reformatory, which is overcrowded and has virtually no programs. A complete guide to programs and institutions in New York is contained in "Social and Health Agencies of New York City," published by Columbia University Press.

Dismissals through The Youth Council Bureau and The Manhattan Court Employment Project are usually arranged when the cases are in Part 3. These are discussed in detail in Chapter 5. Note that referrals to the Youth Council Bureau should be made before a request for youthful offender treatment (described below) is made.

The other principle difference between youths and adults is that youths between the ages of 16 and 19 at the time of arrest are eligible for "youthful offender" treatment. The effect of being found to be a youthful offender is that the defendant, by definition, has not been convicted of a crime. However, employment forms commonly ask whether the applicant has been convicted of a crime or found to be a youthful offender, and, since Y.O.'s are fingerprinted upon conviction, and the records, although theoretically sealed, are in fact open to anyone who is interested, being found to be a Y.O. can have an effect upon a career. The primary advantages of youthful offender treatment are that in serious cases it does somewhat increase the likelihood of probation as opposed to a jail sentence, and if the defendant is rearrested and his prior record consists of nothing but a Y.O. conviction, he can take the witness stand and answer "no" to the question of whether he has ever been convicted of a crime, which is the only question regarding priors that can be asked. Y.O. adjudication also cannot be a bar to government employment or a license of any kind.

Under the old law the determination of whether an accused was to be granted youthful offender treatment was made prior to trial or the entry of guilty plea. The new law, Article 720 of the C.P.L., provides that the sentencing judge decides both the sentence and whether the convicted youth is to receive Y.O. treatment. Under the old procedure the probation department often had to prepare both a pre-pleading and a pre-sentencing report; the new procedure eliminates one of those reports. It also has the effect of inserting the question of Y.O. status into the plea bargaining process. See Chapter 10. By this I mean that in discussing a plea with a judge and/or Assistant District Attorney, you should seek, in addition to other concessions, an agreement by the judge to grant Y.O. treatment, or, if you are in Criminal Court and dealing only with an A.D.A., his agreement to recommend Y.O.

A youth accused of a misdemeanor in Criminal Court, who has not previously been convicted of a crime or adjudicated a Y.O., must be granted Y.O. upon conviction. Section 720.20-1(b). In such a case the court need not order a pre-sentence report' and sentence (most likely probation) can be imposed immediately upon conviction. The new law, § 720.25(b), also provides that this class of youths (alleged misdemeanants with prior convictions or Y.O. adjudications) cannot receive jail sentences of over 6 months. Therefore, since the Supreme Court's rulings in *Duncan v. Louisiana*, 391 U.S. 145 (1968) and *Baldwin v. N.Y.*, 399 U.S. 66 (1970) require a jury trial only where the sentence could exceed 6 months, the legislature was legally able to and did deprive youths in the above-described class of their right to a jury trial. § 340.40(7). This is a severe blow to the defense of youth cases since juries are much more likely than judges to acquit young first offenders accused of misdemeanors. Stating that the defendant does not want Y.O. treatment will not help since § 720.20(b) directs that the court must find such persons to be youthful offenders. If a youth has two open cases, and it appears that he will have to plead guilty to one of the cases, a jury trial can be obtained for the remaining case by first pleading guilty to the other case (of course a better resolution, usually possible, is to plead guilty to one charge to cover both). Note that prior conviction of a violation is not conviction of a crime and Y.O. laws do not apply at all to violations.

Where a youth is eligible for Y.O. treatment—i.e., he has no prior felony convictions, but he has priors and is not automatically entitled to Y.O.—the court will direct that a pre-sentence be prepared by the probation department. The case is adjourned for sentencing and, unless otherwise directed, the judge sitting in that part on the day of sentencing will be the judge who imposes sentence. See Chapter 12 for a more detailed discussion. In preparing pre-sentence reports the probation department sends letters to employers, schools, and references. In difficult cases you can help the defendant to obtain Y.O. treatment and a light sentence by getting anyone who knows the defendant and whose opinion carries some weight to write to the probation officer who is preparing the report. Letters from social workers, clergymen or former employers are helpful; such letters should contain a statement of the context in which the writer knows the defendant, how well he knows the defendant, and his opinion of the defendant's character. The sentencing procedure is the same as for adults, described in Chapter 12, except that the judge also decides, in his discretion, whether to grant or deny Y.O. treatment. As with adults, defense attorneys cannot examine the probation report, although sometimes the judge will informally permit defense counsel to read parts of the report at the bench. If there is any discrepancy between your statements and the report, or if certain crucial factors have changed since the report was written (such as defendant's participation in some kind of program), you should request that the matter be referred back to the probation department for further investigation or updating.

Youths, like anyone else accused of a misdemeanor, are entitled to preliminary hearings. § 170.75. Otherwise motions and trials for youths are handled exactly the same as for adults, with the exception that youths without priors are entitled only to a one-judge trial.

Some special factors to be considered in trying cases involving youths are that those of poor background are often very vague in describing the events of their arrests. They will tell you that the cop found drugs on them, but many do not know that there are rules against searches so they leave out all the facts concerning the search. Youths have to be questioned very carefully and court processes and rules of law have to be explained in detail. Also, many believe that missing a court appearance is no more serious than being absent from school. They have to be told to be sure to appear in court, regardless of excuses, and a call or visit the morning of the court appearance is often necessary. Many youngsters are more afraid of their parents than of the court, and you will not get the true facts out of them unless you speak to them without their parents in the room. Other boys or girls who witness arrests are often reluctant to come to court, or their parents forbid it, for fear that they themselves will get into trouble. A visit to the home of a witness to assure his or her parents is sometimes helpful.

Nowhere is the failure of the Criminal Court to positively effect human behavior more in evidence than in its dealings with youths. There is no job training, rehabilitative schooling, or meaningful supervision. The Youth Council Bureau is meant for those who do not really need help, like the pot smokers or joy riders. A sentence of probation results in the defendant seeing a probation officer for a few minutes once per week for a couple of months, and later once per month. With their large caseloads, probation officers can do no more than refer probationers to other agencies. Jail, of course, is designed to be the ultimately destructive process. The only really good program is the Manhattan Court Employment Project, which handles only a small percentage of the cases.

Chapter 9

REPRESENTATION OF
DRUG ADDICTS

There are two fundamental topics that must be understood by those who represent addicts: the law regarding commitment to the Narcotics Addiction Control Commission, and the voluntary private drug treatment program scene, including both the manner of admission and treatment in the programs and the effects in the court of participation in a program.

Section 200 et. seq. of the Mental Hygiene Law provides in detail the procedures and grounds for certification to the New York State Narcotics Addiction Control Commission (NACC). It is recommended that you read the text of this law before handling cases in this area, particularly since the statute sets forth the procedures regarding certification in great detail. The statute provides for three kinds of certification to the NACC: (1) purely civil certification for persons who are not accused of a crime and who do not have any criminal cases pending, where the medical examination is ordered by the court on the basis of the addict's own petition or the petition of a friend, member of the family, or member of the community; (2) what I call criminal certification, which the statute mandates for persons convicted of misdemeanors who have been found to be addicts, and which is optional for persons found to be addicts, who have been convicted of a felony; (3) civil certification upon the petition of a person accused of a misdemeanor or felony who is certified upon examination by the NACC to be an addict, and which results in dismissal of the misdemeanor charges. The sentence is for a period of up to three years, except for convicted felons, in which case the sentence is up to five years. In practice the NACC keeps addicts in custody for a period of about nine months to one year, and after his release he is placed on a strict parole during which time he must submit to tests for drug addiction. The difference between "civil" and "criminal" certification (all procedures are legally termed "civil") is that criminal certification often leads to the addict actually being sent to a prison. There the only difference between the NACC inmate and other prisoners is that the addict can if he so desires attend group therapy sessions, which are often run by inexperienced personnel. Civil certification results in confinement in considerably better institutions which resemble motels more than jails, although they are locked.

Most knowledgeable people who have taken a close look at the NACC program have concluded that it is essentially custodial in nature and a failure. Especially for criminally certified defendants, certification to the NACC is not significantly different from prison. When the program was first set up, inmates were shackled while being transported. The program has always been regimented somewhat like a prison; the guards are of typically low quality; there is a shortage of trained personnel; and the therapy programs are often run by inadequately trained therapists whose only qualification is a college degree. Most graduates of the program that I have spoken to say that they did not like the program and that they did not find it helpful. The addicts themselves usually resist being committed to the NACC; they believe that the "Rockefeller" program is a bad trip, generally amounting simply to more time in custody than would result from a misdemeanor jail sentence. See *Blunt v. NACC*, 58 Misc. 2d 57, 295 N.Y.S. 2d 276 (Spec Term, Bronx, 1968), in which the court criticized the treatment given by the NACC but denied a writ of habeas corpus by finding that, although the treatment was inadequate, there was some treatment. See also *People v. Murphy*, 55 Misc. 2d 275, 285 N.Y.S. 2d 198, aff'd, 30 App. Div. 2d 358, 293 N.Y.S. 2d 567 (1967), where the court held, among other things, that an addict does not win the right to release in the event that treatment is inadequate. See also *Smoake v. Marrow*, 58 Misc. 2d 266, 294 N.Y.S. 2d 586 (1968), where the court held that the Woodbourne Rehabilitation Center was not a correctional institution, but that inadequacy of treatment does not create a right to release.

When a drug addict is arrested, the arresting officer, if he notices symptoms, fills out a "CR1" form on which he notes the signs of drug addiction that he observes, such as drowsiness, runny nose, needle marks, and, later on, nausea and vomiting, etc., and any statements made by the defendant concerning his drug use. This form is attached to the court papers and given to the judge at the time of arraignment. If the defendant is showing some signs of addiction, the court may order a medical examination pursuant to Section 207 of the Mental Hygiene Law, although very often, perhaps because of the speed of the proceedings, examinations are not ordered for persons who actually are addicts. If, in your conversation with the defendant before arraignment, the defendant denies addiction and the symptoms checked on the form are ambiguous (such as drowsiness and runny nose, which can mean that the defendant is tired and has a cold) then you should object to the order of a medical examination and state for the record your own observations of the defendant's physical condition. You can even request that there be a hearing on this subject. The judge will certainly not grant your request for a hearing and probably will order the medical examination, but he may do something for you by setting a low bail and allowing the defendant to be examined while not in custody. Although most examinations are done while defendants are in custody (the examination must be done within approximately 72 hours of the time of arrest in order for certain of the tests of addiction to be accurate), the court must set a bail and can grant parole or a bail that the defendant can meet, and the defendant may be ordered to submit to the medical examination when he is not in custody. If the latter occurs, the arrestee will be given an appointment slip for the medical examination right after the arraignment.

Commitment to the NACC can only be ordered by the court after the defendant has been "certified" to be an addict by a physician of the NACC, following a medical examination. An exception to this rule is that where the defendant can testify as to his addiction, and the court can then make a finding of addiction and commit. Not infrequently judges order medical exami-addiction, and the court can then make a finding of addiction and commit. Not infrequently judges order medical examinations at some later date when the defendant is not in custody and he appears before the court with symptoms of addiction, such as drowsiness and watery eyes. Some judges even revoke bail to get the suspected addict off the street. Section 207-1 provides that "Such medical examination shall take place with all reasonable speed after the person is arrested or brought before the court." Subdivision 3 of Section 207 further provides that where a person is released on bail or parole, *the judge before whom he first appears* after his release shall order the examination at a specified date and time. Although the language of this section is not completely clear, it does appear that a medical examination cannot be ordered at the second or third court appearance following release. If you make this argument, be prepared with a copy of the statute; almost all judges believe that they have the power to order medical examinations at any time.

The medical examination, according to persons who have submitted to it, is very perfunctory and consequently often inaccurate. It begins with the doctor questioning the person being examined on whether he is an addict, how much he uses per day, how long he has used it, and his method of administering the drug to himself. Unfortunately, many arrestees, believing that they will receive treatment for their drug addiction from a physician, openly admit the facts about their drug use. The doctors of course do not inform the arrestees of what will happen to them if they are found to be addicts. If you are handling a case which continues to a point at which such statements are introduced against your client at a trial on the question of his drug addiction (which is specifically authorized by Section 207), you should object to them on the basis of *Miranda*, which will be opposed by the D.A. with the absurd argument that the proceedings are civil in nature. Lower court decisions have so far held that *Miranda* does not apply to doctors' interviews. *In re Spadafora*, 54 Misc. 2d 123, 281 N.Y.S. 2d 923, *aff'd*, 29 App. Div. 2d 742, 288 N.Y.S. 2d 588 (1967). The doctors also examine the arrestee for needle marks and tracks (a series of needle marks close together creates a track), but these can be from drugs other than heroin, such as amphetamine. The more reliable tests for the presence of heroin, such as urine tests, are generally not administered. Upon completion of the examination, the doctor certifies that the subject is or is not an addict and the arrestee is given a copy of the medical report and certification. If the arrestee is found not to be an addict, then the case continues as would any other.

The criminal prosecution and defense of persons certified by the NACC to be an addict continues in the same way as any other case, except that it must always be kept in mind that conviction, either after trial or upon a plea of guilty, will lead to a commitment to the NACC for up to three years.

After conviction or just before entry of a guilty plea, (which, unless the D.A. waives the finding of addiction, seems senseless since there is nothing to be gained from pleading), a person who has been certified by the NACC to be an addict will be informed by the court that he has the right to admit, deny, or stand mute on the question of his addiction; that if he admits addiction or is found to be an addict after a trial on this question, he will be committed to the custody of the NACC for a period of up to three years, and that he has a right to a jury trial or to a trial before a judge on the question of his addiction. He will then be formally asked for the record whether he is an addict. If he answers no or stands mute, you will be asked whether he wants a trial by jury or a trial before a judge on the issue of his addiction. The decision of whether to have a jury depends on the circumstances of the defendant. The waiting period for a jury trial is now several months, and, therefore, if the defendant is incarcerated, this waiting period, which he will have to spend in one of the more crowded detention facilities, will be intolerable. On the other hand, if he is out of jail and trying to get into a program, the delay can be advantageous. A third consideration is that juries are not generally sympathetic to addicts; most trials before juries on the question of addiction have resulted in verdicts against defendants. Keep in mind that the court can, after conviction, remand a defendant to jail, without bail, pending the drug addiction hearing. However, this will not be done if the defendant is doing something about his drug problem and you can report to the court that he is in a program, in the process of being admitted to a program, or under some form of treatment.

One of the difficulties in representing drug addicts is that most of them go right back to drugs when they get out of jail and they are very likely to be rearrested. Many are arrested three or four times within short periods of time and of course it is practically impossible to prevent someone with so many cases from being sent away. Many addicts, particularly the younger ones, have no understanding of the court processes and are afraid that they will be put in jail at some preliminary stage of the court proceedings. Since they are afraid of jail and the withdrawal systems they will go through if they are put in jail, many young addicts do not show up at their court appearances. There is little you can do other than telling the defendant that you will inform him prior to any court appearance in which there is a chance that he will be put in jail.

The magic works in the criminal court when representing drug addicts are "drug program." Programs looked upon with particular favor are the residential treatment programs using encounter-type group therapy as the main method of treatment. **Methadone and other drug maintenance programs, and even, on** occasion, nonresidential once-per-week encounter programs are also looked upon by the court as substitutes for jail. Anyone who intends to work in this field should visit one of the residential treatment programs and find out about the processes of admission and treatment from the residents so that you can prepare your client for what they will find. Like every rehabilitation program in New York City, the residential treatment centers are crowded and difficult to gain admission into. For most of them, there is a rigorous selection process consisting of numerous appointments, requiring the applicant to perform menial tasks on the premises, and generally giving him a hard time in order to weed out those who are not really motivated. You should prepare your client for this ordeal, but you should also tell him that if he achieves the goal of admission into a program, he will be able to live in a place with persons of similar background, including members of the opposite sex, which he will enjoy living at. Also, through the treatment in the program he will gain insights into himself, conquer his craving for drugs, and possibly acquire the valuable skill of being able to work with other addicts.

On rare occasions for first offenders accused of possession of small amounts, dismissals can be won by the defendant participating in a program. See Chapter 5C.

Where the defendant has been certified by the NACC to be an addict, most of the judges take the position that upon conviction they must commit him to the custody of the NACC where the defendant either admits or is found after trial to be an addict. The judges do not believe that the statute gives them the power to sentence a man to probation, even if he is living in a program. Section 208 of the Mental Hygiene Law supports their view. However, most D.A.s and judges agree that a sentence of probation is indicated where a person is living in a program. The method of achieving this result is that the D.A. concedes non-addiction, despite the finding of addiction by the NACC physician, and the courts accept this practice. Even where a defendant is not living in a residential treatment center, but only participating in an out-patient therapy program, you may be able to achieve the desired result of waiver of the finding of addiction and probation by obtaining a medical report from a private doctor (preferably one who can administer a urine test) indicating that the defendant is off drugs. I suggest that a private doctor be consulted because the NACC examinations are perfunctory and unreliable.

The NACC has the authority to permit persons committed to its custody to actually live in a private voluntary treatment program instead of an NACC facility. See Section 206a of the Mental Hygiene Law. Approval for such an arrangement is rarely given by the NACC unless the addict is in the private program at the time he is committed to the NACC. If he is in a private program the NACC usually lets him stay there. In order for NACC approval to be given, the private program must write a letter to the NACC (at present addressed to Dr. Seymour Josephs, 1855 Broadway, New York, N.Y.) stating that they want to keep the particular person in their program and agreeing to submit periodic progress reports. The NACC will send an investigator to interview the addict and to check on how he is doing in the program, and usually give approval. This process takes four to six weeks and it should be begun long before you expect the commitment to the NACC to take place. If the process is commenced only after commitment, the defendant will probably sit in a prison detention center pending approval. The defendant should be aware that under this arrangement he is actually legally committed to the NACC, and he will be on parole to the NACC when he is discharged from the program.

Also if he quits the program prematurely the NACC will probably take him in.

In very serious cases, like robbery, where the defendant gets into a private program, the court may still not agree to a sentence of probation. A possible compromise between jail and probation is a sentence to the NACC (up to 5 years on a felony) with a transfer to a private program arranged by the program. Of course, you should tell your plans to the court. Most judges will not oppose this disposition since they hold the programs in high esteem, and, in the event of a scandal arising out of a crime committed by that defendant in the future, the judge will not be the one who is accused of being too lenient, which might be the case if he sentenced the defendant to probation.

The trial on the question of addiction is very technical and specialized, involving cross-examination of a physician on questions on the symptoms and signs of drug addiction, the tests for addiction, the accuracy of those tests, the ambiguous meanings of the symptoms and tests, and even questions on the physician's knowledge of the recognized literature in the field. The Legal Aid Society has an excellent manual on how to try cases in this area, written by David Bernheim, entitled *Representing the Convicted Addict in a Hearing to Contest the Finding of Addiction*, but it is still unpublished. A trial on the question of addiction should not be undertaken without first reading this manual and certain portions of the recognized literature in this field, which is mentioned in the manual. The Legal Aid Society has lawyers who are well trained in this field, and, if your client is eligible, the best course of action from the point of view of your client might be to withdraw from the case and have Legal Aid take over.

Section 210 of the Mental Hygiene Law gives a person accused of a misdemeanor or felony who has been certified to be a narcotic addict by a physician of the NACC the right to petition the court, prior to conviction, for a civil certification. Unfortunately, at times the NACC claims that its civil facilities are over-burdened and they ask the court not to accept such petitions, and, the courts, in compliance with statute (§ 210a), refuse to civilly commit on an addict's own petition during such times. The result of such a civil certification is that the defendant will reside in a civil institution and the criminal cases pending against him will be dismissed.

The procedure for obtaining such a civil certification is to obtain from the clerk a petition for civil certification and an order of civil certification upon defendant's petition. The former must be signed by the defendant and the latter will be signed by the judge in court. All of the defendant's cases must be put on the calendar on the same day (if others are on the calendar on other days simply ask the clerk to place them on the calendar on the date that you intend to petition the court). When the case is called you simply inform the court that the defendant is hereby petitioning the court for civil certification pursuant to Section 210 of the Mental Hygiene Law and also moving to dismiss the pending criminal cases in view of the petition for civil certification. The statute gives the judge discretion in granting or denying the petition but it does not contain any guidelines or standards, which may make it unconstitutional if it is ever challenged. Where the defendant is charged with a felony, the consent of the D.A. is required, but many judges also believe, incorrectly, that the D.A.'s consent is required in misdemeanor cases. However, even though the D.A.'s consent is not required in misdemeanors, he can urge the court to exercise its discretion in not granting the petition. If the judge grants the petition, a commitment order is signed on the spot and the criminal cases are dismissed.

Chapter 10

PLEA BARGAINING

The art of plea bargaining, including knowing when to plead, requires knowledge and experience about everything and everybody in the courthouse. In order to decide whether to seek a plea, and to gain the best possible result for your client in a difficult case, you need to know the character and flexibility of the District Attorneys and judges, the likelihood of winning the case in some way, the probable sentence with or without trial, your client's preferences and the possible effects of a plea on him, and so on. Discussion with an experienced practitioner is often necessary. All that this chapter can hope to do is to point out the factors to be weighed in deciding whether to plead, the general practices in plea bargaining, and a brief outline of what kind of plea bargains you can expect.

In considering whether your client should plead guilty, probably the most important question is whether a dismissal can be won in some way or whether an acquittal after trial is possible. Deciding this question involves completely sizing up your case, including such factors as whether the complainant, if a civilian, will continue to show up in court, the testimonial ability of your witnesses as opposed to the witnesses for the State, and of course the general prejudice on the part of the majority of judges in favor of policemen and against persons outside middle-class society. If you come to the conclusion that the case cannot be won, either through a program, on its merits, or by default, then you need go no further and a guilty plea is indicated. This does not mean that you should not wait for an opportune moment to plead. An exception to the above is for certain defendants in political cases who simply, as a matter of principle, will not plead guilty.

Even in the borderline case where a victory might be possible, there are advantages to pleading guilty. For a defendant with a prior record, where a conviction after trial is likely to result in a jail sentence, a guilty plea before a lenient judge, or with an agreement with the judge, can result in a sentence other than jail. Even in a case where there is a good legal argument, a guilty plea for a sentence of no jail time may be preferable for your client since the trial court may not accept your legal argument, and your client might sit in jail while the appeal is pending.

Another important factor, particularly in political and demonstration cases where a plea to a violation is available, is whether the numerous appearances in court are worth the advantage of a possible acquittal at the end of the case. Some groups may think it wiser to plead guilty to a violation at an early stage of the proceedings, especially where there is a waiver of fingerprints, so that they can direct their energies toward the political struggle they are engaged in instead of losing precious time in court. It should be mentioned that when there is a conviction of a violation and a waiver of fingerprints, there is no record of the occurrence other than under the date of arrest and date of conviction, and, of course, it is not a conviction of a crime.

The decision about whether or not to plead guilty should be your client's decision, no matter what his age or understanding of the court processes. When necessary the meaning of a guilty plea must be explained in simple terms and the defendant should be told what he will be asked and what answers make the plea acceptable. Often he or she will look to you for advice on what to do. All you can do is tell him your thought processes on the subject, i.e., that the police officer's testimony will probably lead to a conviction, that the court will not believe that the officer planted drugs, that in view of the fact that the defendant has a prior record, avoiding jail is more likely by pleading guilty and thus picking the sentencing judge, etc. The decision is then the defendant's. In non-political cases, whether the defendant proclaims his innocence is not decisive in my opinion, because he may be lying, and also because the question of guilt or innocence is irrelevant to many people who are caught in the criminal court process. The state legislature's view of what constitutes crime is not shared in the slightest by

103

many people; guilt or innocence of the "crime" becomes meaningless since to many people the acts constituting the crime are not morally wrong. The important consideration becomes whether a guilty plea will untangle the defendant from the court and, for someone with career ambitions, what effect the conviction will have on his future.

Plea bargaining results in agreements between the attorney for the defendant and the District Attorney that the defendant will plead guilty to a lesser charge in satisfaction of all charges pending against him. The quid pro quo in this deal is that the district attorney has the terribly over-burdened calendar cleared of this case without a trial while the defendant, of course, avoids conviction of the more serious charges, and avoids the risk of longer periods of time in jail. Agreement on pleas can generally be made at any stage of the proceeding, from arraignment to trial, although the D.A.'s office is attempting to cut down the number of cases on the calendar and avoid delays by making an offer of a plea at an early stage of the proceeding and telling the defense counsel that this offer will not be made again. Do not be taken in by such threats. The number of cases that are scheduled for trial is always greater than the number of cases that can possibly be tried, particularly now that jury trials are available, and the D.A. must and will plea bargain at later stages. In fact, the plea bargains in the jury part have been very favorable.

In cases where the complainant is a police officer, plea bargaining should begin with talking to the police officer. Find out his version of what took place and his attitudes toward the defendant, and ask him whether he goes along with the disposition of the case that you are seeking. It is important to know what the police officer's attitudes are since the D.A. will almost never agree to a disposition without talking to the officer. It is also important for you to know the general attitudes of the D.A. in the part for that day. Some are completely impossible to deal with, others are more progressive in that they give breaks to defendants who are really showing progress in their own lives, and still others are lenient in almost all cases.

The Legal Aid lawyers can answer your questions about District Attorneys and judges. There may be a more favorable District Attorney in a back-up part and, if you are entitled to a hearing anyway, you can simply have the case marked ready for hearing, sent to the back-up part, and then you can plea bargain with the District Attorney in the back. It is also often more convenient to deal with D.A. in a back-up part anyway, since he will have more time to talk to you. If you cannot reach an agreement, of course, you must then go forward with your hearing.

Occasionally a D.A. will, after evaluating a case and speaking to you, deny your request for a plea to a lesser offense and make a notation on his set of papers that there should not be a plea to a violation or some other lesser offense in this case. Such a notation will probably prevent you from renegotiating the matter with another D.A. "D.A. shopping" is generally frowned upon and most D.A.s will honor notations made by their colleagues.

Trying to persuade the Assistant District Attorney to permit your client to plead guilty to a violation or some other lesser offense is a simple task of salesmanship. You should give him all of the facts that can be persuasive, such as: the defendant's prior record; the minor nature of the crime; the absence of violence; the fact that you are seeking this plea at an early stage of the proceedings; the holes in the government's case; the fact that the trial will be very long and involved and that there will be many pre-trial proceedings; if the defendant has no priors, the fact that the plea you are seeking gives the court adequate scope for sentencing for that kind of crime; the fact that the defendant's behavior and life style have markedly changed since the crime; any programs the defendant is in; and the fact that the plea you are seeking is part of the general practice in the building, or at least that it is not uncommon.

Plea bargaining is generally left to the discretion of the Assistant District Attorney and the judge will almost always go along with any agreement that is reached. Occasionally some judges will call both attorneys to the bench and try to promote an agreement, in which case you must simply tell the judge what you want and why you believe you should get it and hopefully he will agree with you and try to persuade the D.A. to go along.

Sentencing, on the other hand, is the province of the judge, and agreement can sometimes be reached with a judge as to sentence. You must know the judge before seeking a sentencing agreement; many will refuse to discuss the matter, others are such tough sentencers that it is a waste of time to discuss the matter, others are so lenient that it is not necessary and others are so interested in clearing the calendar that such discussions can be very fruitful. The procedure is simply to ask the judge if you can approach the bench with the Assistant District Attorney, then go up to him and tell him that your client will plead to a particular offense (usually a misdemeanor, since agreements on violations are often unnecessary) if the court will agree to a particular sentence. As in your discussions with the D.A., you should inform him of all the persuasive facts, although you will have to be brief. The D.A. will sometimes participate in these discussions but usually he will just listen and go along with whatever the judge will agree to. You will of course have to inform the court of the defendant's prior record and, if there is no print sheet accompanying the court papers, the judge may say that he agrees to your disposition if an investigation and sentence or record and sentence (described in the next chapter) confirm what you have told the court. In such a case, the defendant can plead guilty at the time of the agreement, the judge will order an investigation and sentence (which means that a probation report is prepared), or a record and sentence, and a notation will be made on the court papers that on the date of sentencing about one month later the matter is to be referred to that judge. The judge may agree to permit a withdrawal of the plea if he finds that he cannot keep his end of the agreement. Although there is no legal sanction for agreements on sentencing, they are common practice and the agreements are honored by the judges who make them. Even though a sentencing agreement has been reached, the defendant must answer "no" to the question of whether any threats or promises have been made to him to encourage him to plead guilty, which will be asked at the time that he pleads guilty. If the sentencing is adjourned, be sure to note the date and terms of the agreement on your file; on two occasions in cases I have handled, judges had forgotten the terms of the agreement, but they accepted my notes as correct.

There are virtually no hard and fast rules regarding pleading and sentencing agreements. This area perhaps more than any other depends on the particular case, the defendant's past record, what the defendant is doing with his life now, the attitudes of the complainant, how long the case has been pending, how long a trial will be, and whether the state will have difficulty in proving its case. About all that can be said is that for persons with no prior record or a very light prior record, you can generally get a plea to a violation in disorderly conduct or harassment cases where the defendant is also charged with resisting arrest or interfering with governmental administration; or where there are misdemeanor charges arising out of a demonstration; or where there has been a minor assault or trespass; and for possession of marijuana, barbiturates or amphetamines. An occasional D.A. may offer a violation in a light heroin case for a defendant with no priors. The sentence for a first offender who pleads guilty to a violation is almost invariably a conditional or unconditional discharge, or a $25 or $50 fine.

Your client generally will be permitted to plead guilty to a class B misdemeanor in cases involving moderately heavy assaults, simple possession of heroin or LSD or hypodermic instruments, more serious demonstration cases, and generally where the charges consist of class A misdemeanors or certain non-violent felonies, and the defendant has a very small record or none at all. The Assistant District Attorney will generally agree to allow a plea to a class B misdemeanor in any class A misdemeanor case where he does not believe that conviction of the class A misdemeanor would result in a sentence of more than three months. Now that jury trials are available in class A misdemeanor cases, pleas to a class B misdemeanor are offered in many cases even though conviction of the class A would probably mean a sentence of more than 3 months. Of course, where the defendant has no prior record and a jail sentence is unlikely, your client has not gained anything by pleading guilty to a B misdemeanor since it still results in conviction of a crime, fingerprinting is mandatory, and he may be sentenced to probation.

Sentencing agreements are much more common in the Supreme Court than in the Criminal Court and in serious cases, even where there is a possibility of getting a reduction to a misdemeanor in return for a guilty plea in Criminal Court, you can often do better with regard to sentencing in the Supreme Court. The Assistant District Attorneys in the Supreme Court participate much more in the sentencing agreement than their counterparts in Criminal Court. Thus in some felony cases where a plea to a misdemeanor is offered in Criminal Court, but where such a plea would probably mean a jail sentence, it may be advisable to plead in Supreme Court after indictment, where, especially in complicated cases, a sentence of no jail time may be possible. Note that in Supreme Court the plea may have to be to a felony while the Criminal Court can jurisdictionally accept pleas only to misdemeanors. The converse is also true. Depending on the judge and the case, a jail sentence may be less likely without agreement in the Criminal Court than in Supreme Court, where the case is examined more closely.

When a defendant has two or more cases pending at one time and it appears that one or more of these cases are not likely to be won, it is usually advantageous to plead your client to one or more of the cases in return for dismissal of the others. This kind of plea bargaining is common and accepted. Such bargains are beneficial to the defendant in that they reduce the time he is likely to spend in jail since if he goes to trial on all cases and loses he will receive a jail sentence for each case; the state on the other hand has the advantage of having the calendar cleared and a great deal of court time saved, while still sending the defendant away.

When a person has cases pending in both the Criminal and Supreme Courts, you can sometimes work out an agreement whereby the defendant pleads guilty to the felony in Supreme Court and the judge upon sentencing states for the record that he is "taking into account" the Criminal Court case in passing sentence. Such statements have no binding effect on the Criminal Court judges, and there are no laws on the subject. However, as a practical matter, if you produce a transcript of the sentencing proceeding in Supreme Court and the judge has said that he has taken the Criminal Court case or cases into account in passing sentence, you can virtually always either get the Criminal Court charges dismissed, or, upon a plea, get a conditional discharge or sentence that runs concurrently to the Supreme Court sentence.

In the Criminal Court where you have an agreement that the defendant shall plead to one or more cases in satisfaction of several cases, the mechanics are simply to have the court clerk

108

put all the cases on the calendar on the date the plea will be made. No advance notice is needed to accomplish this. However, if the cases are pending in different parts of the courthouse, it may be necessary for the District Attorney to get the papers and tell the clerk to put them on the calendar. The pleas are then taken and the other cases are either dismissed on the spot on motion of the District Attorney, or, if the sentence is adjourned, the other cases are sometimes kept open and dismissed on the date of sentence (the District Attorney will note on his records that the cases are to be dismissed). The reason for this is obvious; the district attorney wants the judge who sentences the defendant to know that the guilty plea covers more than the case in which the plea was given.

The bargains depend on the cases and the defendant's background; there are no rules. It can be one for three, one for four, two for three, two for four, an A and B misdemeanor, a B misdemeanor and a violation, two violations, and so on. Where several persons are arrested, particularly in an apartment or car for possession of drugs, there can also be a plea by one or more defendants in return for a dismissal of the charges pending against the other defendants.

The procedure for pleading guilty is that, if the lesser offense is not included in the complaint, the assistant district attorney moves to add the reduced charge to the complaint. You then inform the court that the defendant wishes to plead guilty to **some particular charge in satisfaction of all charges presently** pending against him. For misdemeanors the Assistant District Attorney must then arraign the defendant. This is done as follows: he first asks the defendant whether he is the person named in the complaint; he informs the defendant that he is charged with a particular offense in that at such and such date, time and place, he did commit the following act, and here he summarizes the facts contained in the complaint; he then asks the defendant how he pleads to that charge and whether he understands that a plea of guilty is the same as a conviction after trial; he asks the defendant whether he understands that by pleading guilty he waives his right to a jury trial, to confront **and cross-examine witnesses against him and to testify on his** own behalf; defendant is also asked whether any threats or promises have been made to him to induce him to plead guilty (to which he must answer "no" even if a deal has been made), if he understands that a plea of guilty can result in a jail sentence of whatever the particular maximum sentence is, and if he is pleading guilty because he is in fact guilty. The questions may be asked in some other order and in different form but the content is essentially accurate. After satisfactory answers, the D.A. recommends acceptance of the plea and the judge will rule whether the plea is acceptable. It is important to prepare your client for these questions; if they are not properly answered, the court will not accept the plea.

When a defendant is pleading guilty to a violation the entire arraignment can be waived by the defense attorney simply stating that the defendant waives formal arraignment. The right to a two-day adjournment of sentencing under the old Code has been dropped, and Section 380.30 of the C.P.L. says only that the court, before pronouncing sentence, must ask the defendant if he wants an adjournment and then the court can in its discretion grant or deny the request. The court will then ask whether there is any legal cause why sentence should not now be imposed and, upon the defense attorney's answer of "no," sentencing will take place on the spot.

Chapter 11
TRIAL

A. Introduction

Almost everything that has ever been written on the subject of trials stresses that the key to success is thorough preparation, and the reader may be bored reading it again. Nevertheless, it deserves repeating. Thorough preparation not only results in the lawyer actually doing a better job in getting all the favorable facts before the court in the best manner, but he will also appear more confident and more convinced of his client's innocence, which is important. Also, if you are thoroughly prepared you will be better able to closely follow the testimony of the state's witnesses, which will mean that you will do a better job in cross-examination.

Many experienced lawyers advise that in big cases it is helpful to prepare a trial book, using either a small looseleaf book or a spiral notebook. It should be indexed with tabs into sections such as opening remarks to jury, cross-examination of state's witnesses, testimony of defense witnesses, evidentiary problems, legal arguments, and summation. The advantages of such a book are that it forces you to organize your work and become more familiar with it, it saves time during the trial, and it gives the court or jury the impression that you are thoroughly prepared, which in itself is influential. Documentary evidence as well as notes should be placed in this book.

The defense attorney must thoroughly know the rules of evidence; judges usually do not. The courts often allow into evidence subjects that they feel are relevant and proper, without much regard for the fine points of the rules of evidence, particularly the hearsay evidence rule and the exceptions to it. By carefully reviewing the subjects on which you intend to question, you can anticipate evidentiary problems and either brief them or come to court with photostats of cases or selected paragraphs from *Bender's New York Rules of Evidence.*

Needless to say, your preparation should include a thorough interviewing of witnesses. Defense witnesses, and the defendant, if he is going to take the stand, should be interviewed at least two or three times in depth prior to trial. You should put them through a thorough cross-examination, as though you were the prosecutor, and you should explain to them that they will be cross-examined in that manner when they are on the witness stand. Many witnesses at first relate skimpy stories and you should bring out all the details and make sure that the witnesses relate these details in their direct testimony. Prosecution witnesses should also be interviewed, as discussed in Chapter 6B.

In preparing for trial, beginners should not hesitate to write out questions in full, both for direct and cross, and, if necessary, to read them in court. You will often find that you will not need to use the questions you have written out, but that having written them out helps you to conduct a smoother extemporaneous cross-examination. Perhaps in addition you can makes notes of the areas in which you want to cross-examine so that at the trial if you desire not to use your written questions, you can simply quickly refer to your notes. An opening statement to the jury, legal arguments, and the summation can likewise be written out in full and read in court if necessary.

My own experience is that the best way to finally prepare for trial is to begin a few weeks before trial and read the file and go over the facts thoroughly on several different occasions, making notes of your ideas each time. I have found that each time I go over a case I have some new ideas, some of which are worthwhile. An additional meeting with the witnesses will also bring out new facts and ideas. The night before trial again go over the file thoroughly and weed out the good ideas from the bad. It is often helpful to discuss the case with a person, not necessarily a lawyer, who knows nothing about the case, in order to put things into perspective. There is a danger that becoming very involved in the facts may lead you to lose sight of the significance, or insignificance of certain events, and a fresh eye on the case cannot hurt.

B. Theory of The Case

The defense of a criminal case should have a basic theory, or perhaps even two theories, and the entire trial should be conducted with that theory in mind. Evidence in support of that theory or theories should be emphasized, and evidence which is damaging to the defendant, but which is not in conflict with the theory of defense should not be refuted so as not to cloud the issue. Examples of such theories are that the state simply fails to prove its case beyond a reasonable doubt; that there is a mistaken identification; that the police officer is lying; that there is no criminal knowledge or intent as required by law; self-defense; and justification. The defense of justification (Section 35.05 of the Penal Law) is that the defendant is not guilty of the crime which he or she actually committed by reason of the fact that the acts were done in order to prevent the commission of a more serious crime or the occurrence of a serious misfortune. Although this statute was probably intended to cover situations such as where a defendant possessed a gun which he took away from someone else who had threatened to commit a murder, the defense of justification can be used to bring out political issues. For example, after the welfare cuts of 1969, many persons were arrested in sit-ins in welfare centers. The defense of justification could have been used to show that the mothers on welfare committed the crime of criminal trespass in order to keep their children healthy and to prevent the much more serious crimes of criminal neglect of their children (since they could not properly feed their children on 66 cents per day), or even petty larceny, which they would be forced to commit in order to have enough food for a healthy diet, etc. Such a theory may not win but it may, in conjunction with other actions, be a good vehicle for publicizing a cause, which may be the most important thing for your clients.

To give another example, where the crime charged is criminal possession of stolen property, and the defense is lack of knowledge that it was stolen, some of the important factors are the behavior of the defendant prior to, during, and following his arrest, the statements made by the defendant prior to and after his arrest, the circumstances as they appeared to the officer and the defendant, and perhaps even the social conditions regarding

113

the availability of the property. Note that there is a case law presumption that possession of stolen property shortly after it is stolen, if unexplained, means that the defendant knew that it was stolen, but this presumption is of course rebuttable. Note also that self-serving statements made by the defendant before and immediately following arrest are admissible despite the fact that they are hearsay (out of court statements offered to prove the truth of the matter asserted therein) under the res gestae exception; courts often do not allow such statements into evidence on the ground that they are self-serving, i.e., not admissions, which is incorrect. Since the defense is lack of knowledge, and possession of the contraband is admitted, the conduct of the arresting officer is not crucial and, unless he leaves out some facts that are favorable to your client, he should not be closely cross-examined and his fellow officer should not be subpoenaed. Likewise, the testimony of the owner of the stolen property need not be cross-examined, unless the time and place that he lost it is important, and in some cases his testimony should even be stipulated to (i.e., conceded).

Judges and D.A.s often put pressure on defense attorneys to try to get them to agree to stipulate to the testimony of a civilian complainant. You should never stipulate to his testimony until he has appeared in court at least once following the arraignment and you have had a chance to talk to him since, if he never appears, the case will be dismissed. If you are pressured, you can avoid appearing to be acting in bad faith by stating that there are several questions that you feel you must ask the complainant (usually a property owner), and that you will be glad to stipulate after you have had a chance to talk to the complainant in the presence of the A.D.A. on the next date that the case is on the calendar. If you examine any case closely, you will usually find that you have some important questions that should be asked of the complainant before stipulating to his testimony. Sometimes civilian owners of property are "placed on telephone call," which means they are told to disregard subpoenas and not appear until they receive a telephone call, and, if they are reliable people, they will in fact appear when called. In such a case nothing is gained by not stipulating, and, in fact it may be better to stipulate to avoid having the court or jury feel sympathetic to the witness. On the other hand, if the civilian owner of property appears to be unreliable, it may be wise not to stipulate at all since if he or she fails to appear at trial, the case must be dismissed. However, failure to stipulate may cause the D.A. to deny your client other breaks, like a reduction to a misdemeanor. In deciding whether to stipulate, you must weigh the advantages against the possible advantages, if any.

Where the defense is lack of knowledge or intent, the defendant should, if at all possible, take the stand and testify as sincerely as he can that he lacked knowledge. Character witnesses, the defendant's life circumstances, and his prior record are very important. These topics are covered in greater detail in subsequent sections of this chapter.

The availability of certain contraband in society may also be relevant to back up a theory of lack of intent. For example, a client of mine was accused of possession of a dangerous weapon when he possessed an ornamental dagger. The statute says that such possession is only illegal where there is intent to use it, but another section of the statute makes possession presumptive evidence of intent to use. The availability of ornamental daggers in antique shops, pawn shops, etc., and their occurrence in society as ornaments is relevant to rebut the presumption and show lack of intent, and also to support an argument that the presumption is illegal since intent to use does not, in the ordinary experience of men, follow from simple possession. An investigation showed that most pawn shops on the Lower East Side sold daggers to anyone who walked in.

C. Deciding Whether to Try The Case Before A Judge or Jury

Deciding whether to try the case before a judge or jury is a very difficult and important decision. Much has been written on this subject but most of it is not completely relevant to misdemeanor trials in New York City, for several reasons. First of all, juries for misdemeanor trials in New York City have 6 members instead of 12 and the judge, not the lawyer, conducts the voir dire. Also, jurors in New York City, especially Manhattan, are more sophisticated than elsewhere and are generally more favorable to defendants. Since juries for misdemeanors have only been available since July, 1970, hard statistics and guidelines cannot be given yet.

Experienced lawyers are in agreement on only a few general rules and guidelines:

1. Juries look more to the totality of the circumstances of the case, and the defendant's background and present activities, than do judges. In a light demonstration case, where your clients are students with clean, middle-class backgrounds, a jury is clearly desirable. On the other hand, in a heroin case where the defendant has a heavy record and it is necessary for him to take the stand, lawyers have traditionally advised against juries. However, time may prove this advice wrong for New York City.

2. When the theory of defense is simply that the state has not proven guilt beyond a reasonable doubt (e.g., the evidence is circumstantial), a jury is preferable.

3. When the theory of defense is that the police officer is lying, but the defendant will not take the stand, a jury trial is better. As mentioned earlier, there have already been a few acquittals in dropsey cases where the defendant lost the motion to suppress and did not take the stand, probably because the jury did not believe that the officer was telling the truth. Most judges, even when they believe that the police officer is lying about the details of the case, will convict because they feel that they should accept the uncontradicted word of a police officer, and they believe that the defendant is guilty of the crime and should be convicted.

4. When in doubt, pick a jury. The overall statistics indicate that juries are more likely to acquit.

Along with these criteria, you must also keep in mind such factors as delay (jury trials are likely to have the longest delays in the future although at the time of this writing the jury parts are not busy), the possibility of a plea, and sentencing. If there may eventually be a plea, it may be better to keep the case in 2B if it is important to have a lenient sentencing judge.

A detailed analysis of how to try a case before a jury is beyond the scope of this book. It would take another book, much longer than this one to cover this subject and this author does not have the experience to write it. The reader is referred to an excellent work on this subject, *Trial Manual for the Defense of Criminal Cases*, by Anthony Amsterdam et. ano. The reader is also advised to spend a few days watching jury trials in both Supreme and Criminal Courts.

D. Cross-Examination

The first thing to realize when formulating cross-examination is that you are not going to be able to "break" the witness. Only Perry Mason is capable of doing that. The best you can do is discredit him by showing bias, inconsistencies, impossibilities, or bad character, but the witness will certainly stick to his or her story. Cross-examination is an art that takes time to learn and observing experienced lawyers can be very helpful. You will, however, have to develop a natural style of your own and you should not try to imitate others.

The first question to ask yourself is whether to cross-examine a witness at all. Inexperienced lawyers often cross-examine when they should not, sometimes with disastrous results. There is a story of a case in which a man was accused of biting off the ear of the complainant and a witness was asked by the prosecutor if he saw this happen, to which the witness answered "no." The defense foolishly asked the witness what he did see, to which the witness replied, "I saw the defendant spit it out." There are also cases in which the witness' direct testimony is so long and detailed that he leaves out some important fact, such as a case where a police officer testified at a preliminary hearing in detail about an arrest he made at a demonstration and he simply forgot to testify about the resistance to the arrest, which he described in the complaint and which constituted the only misdemeanor charge. The initial question is therefore whether the defendant has been hurt by the witness' testimony at all. If not, then you should not cross-examine at all, unless you expect your cross-examination to bring out something favorable to the defendant.

Beware of a trick employed by some prosecutors in jury trials. The prosecutor may know that the direct testimony of his witness will be skimpy and he purposely does not bring out the details, leaving the elaboration and the damaging evidence to come out on cross-examination, where it hurts the defendant more.

The defense lawyer should be listening very carefully to a witness' direct testimony, rather than taking notes, so that he can concentrate his attention on spotting weaknesses and inconsistencies. The following are some of the general purposes of cross-examination, together with a few examples.

1. To show bias or prejudice. For example, where the defendant is a leftist demonstrator and you suspect that the police officer is politically conservative, you can ask the police officer what the demonstration was about, how he feels about college students taking over schools, how he feels about students demonstrating against the war, what he thinks about such students' loyalty to the country, whether he thinks such demonstrators hurt the American cause in Vietnam, whether he demonstrated in support of the war, etc. In other cases you may try to show that the prosecution is motivated by racial prejudice, but be careful; if you try to show this and fail, you look bad. In assault cases the motive for the complaint may be that the parties are personal enemies and that fact should be brought out.

2. To show an interest in the outcome. For example, an accomplice may have been granted immunity or the prosecutor may have promised to recommend a lenient sentence. Or, in a rare case, there may be a civil suit pending, the outcome of which would be influenced by a conviction.

3. To discredit the witness personally. An addict-informer is the easiest to discredit. You can ask him if he ever stole to get money for drugs, and if he would also lie in order to get drugs, and if, as a result of his testimony, he expects to spend less time in jail, and therefore, be able to take drugs sooner. You should also ask him when he first became an addict, how heavy his habit was, what he did for money for these drugs, etc. Witnesses can also be asked whether they have ever been convicted of a crime. You can also ask questions about prior bad acts, which is interpreted broadly. For example, in a police brutality case where the defendant is charged with assaulting an officer, you can ask whether the officer has ever been found guilty of using excessive force by the Civilian

Complaint Review Board of the Police Department. However, if you ask questions about prior bad acts you must have a basis for asking the question.

4. To elaborate on the direct testimony, where the additional details will make the testimony appear more favorable to the defendant. For example, in a case where my client was charged with criminal possession of stolen property, specifically a camera in a case, the owner of the camera testified on direct that he was in the process of unloading his car, placed the camera on the sidewalk next to his car, went upstairs to his apartment, and came back to find the camera missing. Cross-examination showed that it was late at night on a quiet residential street, no one else was around, the car was locked and the lights off when he went upstairs, the camera case was old and dirty, garbage cans were a few feet away, and there were no other belongings on the sidewalk. The elaboration of the direct testimony showed that the camera appeared to be abandoned.

5. To question the witness' powers of observation. By this is meant such factors as eyesight, lighting, speed of events, whether the witness was frightened, the height of the witness compared to the defendant, etc. More on this in the next section of this Chapter.

6. To demonstrate the witness' lack of credibility. For example, in an assault case where the complainant is paranoid to the point where he or she is mentally ill, you can show that his testimony is incredible by leading him on so that he testifies that there is some fantastic conspiracy being plotted against him. The testimony of children can also often be shown to not be credible because they are very suggestible. I once had a case where my client's child testified that the complainant was the one with a knife and on cross-examination she was led on to a point where she testified that there were five or six other women standing with the complainant and that they all had knives. Children also occasionally memorize their testimony, which makes them go through it very quickly in spurts; when a child has memorized his story, you can demonstrate it in court by asking the child to repeat it two or three times, and it will have the same phrasing each time. Testimony can also be impeached through the use of prior

inconsistent statements. These can be in the form of police department records and reports, notations in the memo book, prior testimony at the preliminary hearing, or statements made to you. Where there is a meaningful discrepancy between the testimony at the preliminary hearing and that at trial, the manner of bringing it out is to ask the witness if he remembers testifying at the preliminary hearing held on such and such date, before Judge XYZ, etc., and after he answers "yes," asking him if he remembers saying the following, at which point the minutes of the preliminary hearing are read into the record. The original complaining affidavit may also be a source of inconsistent statements. Also, if a complaint has been made to the Civilian Complaint Review Board, the officer will have had to testify there and the transcript of his testimony should be obtained for possible impeachment purposes.

Occasionally the complainant's testimony will describe an event that is physically impossible, such as the police officer who claims that he saw glassine envelopes change hands at the door to an apartment in a dark hallway, while he was on a stairway landing half a flight away and 40 feet from the door. The impossibility of the police officer's testimony could be demonstrated by having someone, perhaps a law student, visit the scene and testify as to what is visible, or by requesting that the court reconvene itself at the scene. In another case a police officer testified that while he was attempting to turn off a fire hydrant, the defendant prevented him from doing so by trying to get some water in a bucket in front of the hydrant. The impossibility of his testimony was shown by a re-enactment of the position of the parties in the courtroom; it showed that if the defendant was trying to get water he could not have been in the way of the wrench on the hydrant.

The following are some do's and don'ts regarding the form and manner of presentation of questions in cross-examination:

1. Use strong points at the beginning and end of cross-examination.
2. Ask simple questions, preferably with yes, no, or one word answers, so that they are easily understandable and so that a witness who wants to lie might not have the time.
3. Don't let the witness repeat his direct testimony unless you

have a purpose; hearing it twice just reinforces it in the minds of the triers of fact.

4. Never lose your temper. Be firm and even accusatory; but don't lose your cool.
5. Particularly when before a jury, make all of your cross-examination count; all of your questions should demonstrate something favorable to the defendant, in varying degrees; do not cross-examine at random on every aspect of the direct testimony.
6. Do not be hostile to the witness, especially when it is a civilian complaint, unless he is hostile to you. The jury is often likely to identify more with the witness than the defendent. When trying a case before a judge, this is not quite as important, but the judge may get angry at you for abusing the witness.
7. If a witness' response is damaging, quietly drop the subject and pass on to something else without acting perturbed.
8. When you get an answer that is very favorable, stop. Going further may give the witness a chance to cure the damage. You can emphasize the point later on during summation.
9. Build slowly to good points, that is, lay a foundation. Don't plunge into your conclusory question without setting a stage for it. Setting a stage makes the point clearer and more emphatic. For example, if a police officer testifies that he was on a rooftop and observed a sale take place across the street and half a block away, make him recite all the distances separately (eg: height of the building, width of sidewalk, street, other sidewalk, number of buildings and feet per building, etc.), instead of just asking him how far away he was.

When the witness you are cross-examining is a police officer there are some additional points to keep in mind. First of all there is a basic distinction that must be made between police officers who are complainants or witnesses to the crime and those who are investigating or arresting officers. The latter often have little or nothing to testify about, especially when they are just arresting someone on the complaint of someone else. Sometimes, however, the arresting officer's testimony may be extremely important, such as where there has been an identification or confession. In such cases you can expect the police officer to be a hostile witness, and your questioning should be close and detailed, and it should cover all possibilities, on the assumption that police officers will not volunteer any information that might be helpful to your client. When trying a case before a jury, you need not be quite as gentle with a police officer as you would be with a civilian complainant whom the jury might identify with.

Where the police officer is a witness to the crime, or where he is the complainant, your cross-examination should be much the same as for any other witness, with some additions. Where there are two or more police officers your questions should cover a time period broader than the period covered in the direct testimony, beginning before and ending after the arrest, since, when police officers rehearse their testimony, they sometimes forget to cover those periods. As mentioned earlier, police testimony should also be compared with other records for sources of possible prior inconsistent statements. His memorandum book should be examined (which can only be done after his direct testimony), and the police records of the complaint and arrest should be subpoenaed. See Chapter 6C. These records should be subpoenaed as early as possible and examined prior to trial. Since these records are ordinary business records kept by the police department, rather than only a prior statement of the officer, you are entitled to see these records prior to trial.

Police testimony can also be attacked on collateral matters, such as their failure to reduce an oral confession to writing, failure to conform to their own regulations, beatings, etc. For example, where an oral confession is described by a police officer, and he has not put it in writing, ask him how long he has been on the police force, whether he knows of a regulation that says that oral confessions should be reduced to writing, how long he knows of that regulation, whether he had a typewriter and paper at the time he heard the confession in the police station, how much time he spent with the defendant after the confession, whether he had time to put the confession in writing, whether he prepared other documents that night (which, if you have them, can be enumerated), whether he has heard other confessions over the years, whether he generally obeys the regulation and puts the confession in writing (any answer to this question makes him look bad).

E. Eye Witness Identification

There are many cases in which practically the only issue is the validity of an eye witness identification. In all such cases a hearing should be held on a motion to suppress the identification (a Wade Hearing) (see Chapter 7E). Even if the motion has no chance of success, the hearing is enormously valuable as a discovery device. You will learn how much of a look the complaining witness got of his assailant at the time of the crime, the reliability of his testimony (e.g.: his age, eyesight, emotional condition, and how certain the complainant is about the identification), and how convincing the complainant is as a witness. The hearing will be invaluable in preparing for trial; you will learn the answer to almost all the questions you will ask at trial, and you will learn what areas to probe and what areas to avoid. A Wade Hearing may also move your client toward a plea, or alter his previous decision to plead guilty.

When conducting the trial of such a case there are several factors that must be closely examined which are not present in other cases. Of great importance is the earliest description communicated to the police, including dress, overall appearance, and major features. If it differs from the defendant's actual description, or if it omitted some prominent feature, the complainant's testimony is considerably weakened. The circumstances of the lineup or showup, if suggestive, should also be thoroughly exposed (see Chapter 7E). If there was a showup, you should ask where it was, who was present, what condition the defendant was in, what was done to the defendant (was he handcuffed, ordered about by the police, held by the arm as though he was a prisoner, etc.), what was said by everyone present, and how long did the complainant hesitate before identifying the defendant, etc. If the defendant was first identified by a photograph, and if the photograph is not a good likeness, or if the photographic identification was suggestive because there were too few photographs of people with the defendant's general description, then those facts should be brought out. On the other hand, if the photographic identification was not suggestive, then you should not delve into it, since the state will not be able to introduce evidence of a photographic identification unless you do. *Peo. v. Cioffi*, 1 N.Y. 2d 70, 150 N.Y.S. 2d 192 (1956); *Bender's New York Rules of Evidence*, §151.02.

If there was a suggestive lineup, which can be shown in many cases, you should bring out all the details about it in the manner described in Chapter 7E. Consider subpoenaing the other members of the lineup to demonstrate its suggestiveness in court. This might be especially valuable where the general description of the other members of the lineup is similar to the defendant's, but where the other members are police officers and have a cleaner and straighter look about them than the defendant. Note that the investigation into this first identification after the crime is not for the purpose of excluding it as a violation of due process (which would have been decided at the Wade Hearing), but in order to show that there is a reasonable doubt about the accuracy of the witness' identification of the defendant as his assailant.

The other critical occurrence that has to be investigated is the opportunity the complainant had to view his assailant at the time of the crime. How long did he view the assailant, did he have to look down to find his money or remove jewelry, did he look his assailant in the eye, does he look anyone who speaks to him including yourself in the eye or does he look away to other sections of the room, what were the lighting conditions, how good are his eyes, is he white and his assailant black and if so do all blacks look alike to him, was the perpetrator wearing a hat at the time, how much taller or shorter than his assailant is he, how was his assailant dressed, was he frightened or nervous, etc. Again, you are trying to show that the witness' in court identification of the defendant as his assailant is simply wrong, or that there is a reasonable doubt about its validity.

A relatively simple tactic that can be used to cast doubt on a witness' ability to recollect is to cross-examine on other things surrounding the crime. If the crime occurred in a room or store, or on the street, failure of the witness to remember details about the surroundings will cast some doubt on his or her ability to remember anything. Experienced lawyers tell marvelous stories of more dramatic tactics which they have used to cast doubt on an identification. One lawyer describes a tactic he uses on a witness who is nervous and who avoids looking at his interrogator; he wears a loud tie and then in the middle of his questioning, he turns around, covers his tie with his lapels, and asks the witness what color tie he is wearing. The jury will all know and if the witness does not, he has scored a few points. A former defense lawyer and teacher, who is now a judge, tells of a case where the delay between arrest and trial was long and the complainant had not seen the defendant for a long time, and the defendant was a derelict. He cleaned the derelict up, got him a shave, haircut, and good suit of clothes, and he had his law partner let his hair and beard grow and put on the derelict's clothes. Both sat at the defense table and the complainant pointed to the lawyer when asked to identify his assailant. The problem with using tactics like this is that if they do not work you will look foolish and your client will be hurt, so use them cautiously.

F. Should the Defendant Take the Stand

The question of whether the defendant should testify on his own behalf is one of the most difficult questions facing a trial lawyer. On the one hand if he does not testify, both judge and jury undoubtedly draw inferences of guilt, despite law and instructions to the contrary. On the other hand, where the defendant will be a bad witness or where he has a long record, it is often wiser for him not to testify. In many cases the defense can be adequately made out without him taking the stand, while in others, particularly where the evidence is circumstantial, there is a better chance for success merely by submitting the question of reasonable doubt, based on the state's case, to the jury. On the other hand, when trying a case before a judge my experience has been that if the defendant does not take the stand and a barely adequate case is made out, a judge will convict. It is of course impossible to make guidelines in this area, but the beginner should keep in mind that most experienced lawyers agree that there have been many cases where the prosecution's case was weak and there was a chance for an acquittal, but the defendant's testimony, because of its vagueness, or holes, or manner of presentation, convicted him.

Many lawyers are under the mistaken assumption that as soon as the defendant takes the stand his entire criminal record can be used to impeach him. There is a considerable body of law to the contrary in New York and priors have been excluded because they were not indicative of deceitfulness, or not at all related to the offense charged, or because their admission into evidence would have been too prejudicial to the defendant. See *Abbott's Digest*, Volume 6a, Criminal Law, § 369 et. seq., for cases on this subject. If you have a problem like this, probably the best way to handle it is to make a formal motion to exclude priors, on papers, supported by a brief, and returnable some day that the case is on the calendar but prior to the date of actual trial.

The theory in this area is well stated in an opinion written by now Chief Justice Warren Burger in the case of *Gordon vs. U.S.*, 383 F2d 936, at 938 (D.C. Cir. 1967):

"In considering how the District Court is to exercise the discretionary power we granted, we must look to the legitimate purpose of impeachment which is, of course, not to show that the accused who takes the stand is a 'bad' person but rather to show background facts which bear directly on whether jurors ought to believe him rather than other and conflicting witnesses. In common human experience acts of deceit, fraud, cheating, or stealing, for example, are universally regarded as conduct which reflects adversely on a man's honesty and integrity. Acts of violence on the other hand, which may result from a short temper, a combative nature, extreme provocation, or other causes, generally have little or no direct bearing on honesty and veracity. A 'rule of thumb' thus should be that convictions which rest on dishonest conduct relate to credibility whereas those of violent or assaultive crimes generally do not; traffic violations, however serious, are in the same category. The nearness or remoteness of the prior conviction is also a factor of no small importance. Even one involving fraud or stealing, for example, if it occurred long before and has been followed by a legally blameless life, should generally be excluded on the ground of remoteness.

"A special and even more difficult problem arises when the prior conviction is for the same or substantially the same conduct for which the accused is on trial. Where multiple convictions of various kinds can be shown, strong reasons arise for excluding those which are for the same crime because of the inevitable pressure on lay jurors to believe that 'if he did it before he probably did so this time.' As a general guide, those convictions which are for the same crime should be admitted sparingly; one solution might well be that discretion be exercised to limit the impeachment by way of a similar crime to a single conviction and then only when the circumstances indicate strong reasons for disclosure, and there the conviction directly relates to veracity.

"Of course, there are many other factors that may be relevant in deciding whether or not to exclude prior convictions in a particular case. See (*Luck v. United States*, 348 F.2d 763 [D.C. Cir. 1965], at 769. One important consideration is what the effect will be if the defendant does not testify out of fear of being prejudiced because of impeachment by prior convictions. Even though a judge might find that the prior convictions are relevant to credibility and the risk of prejudice to the defendant does not warrant their exclusion, he may nevertheless conclude that it is more important that the jury have the benefit of the defendant's version of the case than to have the defendant remain silent out of fear of impeachment . . ."

G. Character Witnesses

Character witnesses can be helpful when they know the defendant or his reputation well and when they are of high enough stature, to the jury or judge, to carry some weight. Where the defendant is young, perhaps a teacher, principal, social worker, or counselor can be found who will testify on the defendant's behalf. Note that the character witness must know the defendant's reputation in the community, and, in theory, he can only testify as to that reputation, not as to his own opinion of the defendant. The basic questions that must be put to the character witness are: Have you had occasion to discuss the defendant's reputation in the community, do you know his reputation in the community, and what is that reputation in the community. The witness may then be cross-examined on the discussions he has had about the defendant's reputation, and a possibly troublesome point in some cases is that the witness may also be asked whether he knows of certain prior bad acts of the defendant. Thus, having a character witness testify may bring out prior bad acts which would otherwise not have become known to the trier of fact.

The principle flaw in the manner of presentation of most character witnesses' testimonies are that they are not sufficiently embellished. Wherever suitable the witness should be encouraged to go into detail about his own background, education, job record, any books he has written, family life, etc. He should then go into detail about how well he knows the defendant, the exact context in which he knows him, how often he has seen him, whether he has been to the defendant's home, whether he knows his family, whom he has spoken to about his reputation, whether he has ever evaluated the defendant's behavior for some kind of report, etc. When asked about the defendant's reputation, the witness should be encouraged to give a one or two sentence answer, giving specific character traits, rather than simply saying that the defendant's reputation is good or excellent.

H. Admission of Evidence

The law regarding what is and is not admissible into evidence is much too complicated for this manual. The reader is referred to *Abbott's Digest*, Volume 6a, Section 304 et. seq. for New York cases, and *Bender's New York Rules of Evidence*, or any other treatise on evidence. All that will be set forth in this section are the procedures and magic words for getting things into evidence.

Generally speaking, a foundation must be laid for any piece of evidence before it can be admitted. That is, its relevance and relationship to the case must be shown. If you wish to refer to something before it is admitted into evidence, particularly in order to lay a foundation for its admittance into evidence, the procedure is to request that the item be marked "defendant's exhibit X for identification." For example, if a witness is testifying and you have a letter signed by that witness which you wish to introduce into evidence, the proper procedure would be to pick up the letter, announce that you wish to have this letter, dated such and such, with letterhead from such and such company, addressed to so and so, marked defendant's exhibit X for identification. The court reporter will then physically mark it. You can then show it to the witness and ask if that is his signature, if he signed that letter, and if that letter refers to a particular relevant topic. After the witness answers affirmatively, you say: "Your honor, I request that this letter be admitted into evidence as defendant's exhibit Y in evidence." The District Attorney may object at this time and the judge will rule whether the evidence is to be admitted. If it is admitted, it is given to the court clerk and physically marked "defendant's exhibit Y in evidence." You can then ask the witness whether it is not a fact that on such and such date he wrote a letter to so and so in which he stated the following, and then you can read the letter and show it to the jury.

Photographs must generally be identified by the person who took the photograph as a fair and accurate representation of what he saw at the time and place that the photograph was taken, and the manner of development and the possessor of the photograph from the time it was taken until the time it was presented into court must be revealed in order to rule out tampering. The same is true for moving pictures, which present more of a problem because they can be spliced. If the case is being tried before a jury, the court will generally view the entire motion picture before ruling on its admissibility. Again, there is case law on this subject which should be researched.

When you are impeaching a witness with a prior inconsistent statement, such as his testimony at a preliminary hearing, the procedure is as follows: First ask the witness if he remembers testifying at a preliminary hearing held on such and such date before judge XYZ, and then ask whether he remembers saying the following, and then you simply read the relevant portions of the transcript, both questions and answers. The District Attorney will undoubtedly stipulate to the accuracy of the transcript to avoid the court reporter having to testify to its accuracy, which wastes everybody's time.

Where the item you are seeking to introduce into evidence is an official record or document of some kind, which is obviously valid on its face, such as a stamped automobile registration, the district attorney will generally stipulate to its validity to avoid a government official having to be subpoenaed and to avoid an adjournment for that purpose.

Note that evidence of an insanity defense may not be admissible unless 30 days' notice of intent to introduce such a defense is given to the Court and D.A. § 250.10. Somewhat similarly the state may demand that the names and addresses of alibi witnesses, and the nature of the alibi claimed, be disclosed and failure to do so may make the evidence inadmissible, unless a good excuse is given. § 250.20.

I. Summation and Motions

When trying a case before a jury the summation is a very important and often lengthy speech. It is very simply an argument to the jury that they should acquit because your general theory of the case is correct. The key word is "sincerity." You should emphasize every piece of testimony and evidence in favor of your client and you should also mention the evidence against your client, and try to either distinguish it, point out its unreliability or ambiguity, or, if it is really definitely against your client, admit to its unfavorability. That will demonstrate your sincerity.

Making a good summation speech is a very sophisticated art. You are again referred to Prof. Amsterdam's work, cited in the beginning of this chapter, and again it is helpful to watch experienced lawyers in action. Briefly it can be added that any jury summation should emphasize the concepts of reasonable doubt, burden of proof, and, where applicable, the prohibition against drawing any inference whatsoever from the defendant's failure to take the stand. Where potentially favorable witnesses have failed to appear the reason should be stated to the jury, since the prosecution will probably cite their non-appearance. The jury should also be reminded that they must bring in the verdict that they as individuals feel is correct.

When trying a case before a judge or judges the summation should not be lengthy. You can run down the evidence and comment on it, but, since trials before judges are usually short, they will not have patience with a long speech that reiterates testimony they have just heard. You can, however, comment on why particular witnesses did not appear, and on the failure of the state to produce certain witnesses, and on factors such as credibility.

In trials before judges there are very few customary motions to be made. At the close of the state's case, it is customary to make a motion to dismiss for failure of the state to make out a prima facie case, whether or not it stands any chance of success. At the close of the trial, your motion is to acquit for failure of the state to establish the defendant's guilt beyond a reasonable doubt. For samples of the wording of many other motions that are made, see *Complete Manual of Criminal Forms* by F. Lee Bailey and Henry B. Rothblatt, Lawyers Cooperative Publishing Co., Rochester, N.Y.

Roughly the same is true when trying a case before a jury. At the close of the state's case, the customary motion is for a dismissal for failure of the state, as a matter of law, to introduce enough evidence upon which a conviction can be based. After both sides have rested, the motion is for a directed verdict of acquittal, or dismissal before submission to the jury, on the grounds .that, as a matter of law, the state has not proven the defendant guilty beyond a reasonable doubt. An oral argument can be made in support of these motions.

At the close of the trial, after verdict but before judgment (sentence) is imposed, a motion to set aside the verdict can be made on any one of a number of grounds, as set forth in § 330.30 of the C.P.L. Lawyers commonly make a perfunctory motion to set aside the verdict on the grounds that it is contrary to the evidence or contrary to law, but the motion can also be based on any appealable issue or error in the trial, improper conduct by a juror (e.g., reaching a verdict by lot, or visiting the scene), new evidence not known during the trial, improper instructions, impermissible remarks by the prosecutor, etc. See *Abbott's New York Digest* Vol. 7, § 905 et. seq. After sentence a motion to vacate the judgment may be made to the sentencing court, as described in § 440.10. The reader is referred to Article 440 of the C.P.L. for an enumeration of the permissible grounds, rules, and procedures for making such a motion.

Chapter 12

SENTENCING

An attorney should consider sentencing problems at the first conference he has with his client. If the case is one which, considering the defendant's prior record, may result in a jail sentence, a client should be advised that if he wants to stay out of jail he should prepare for sentencing immediately by beginning to do something such as going to school, working, or entering a program of some kind. Of course there are people, notably young politically active people, who do not wish to change their life styles and prefer to take their chances of getting jail sentences. Your job is merely to inform them that the court is an institution with middle-class American values and that when the lawyer cannot tell the judge that his client is doing something which the court views as constructive, sentencing is likely to be stiffer. You and your client are of course in no position to alter the court's values from your side of the bench.

There are several different time periods following conviction when sentencing can take place. It can be immediately after conviction, or be put off from a few days to two weeks later for a "record and sentence," or four to eight weeks later for an "investigation and sentence," or sentence can be deferred for three or six months or even longer when the judge is waivering between probation and a jail sentence and wants the defendant to prove himself before he is permitted to remain out of jail.

The right to a two-day adjournment under old C.C.P. has been abolished and § 380.30 of the C.P.L. leaves it up to the judge whether to grant or deny an adjournment between conviction and sentence. In minor cases, such as violations, or where the defendant has no prior record, or where a deal is made on the sentence, or in any case where the defendant's yellow sheet is present and no useful purpose is served by adjourning, the defendant can be sentenced on the spot. This is particularly advantageous when you are before a lenient judge or where certain other facts, depending on the case, may appear if there is an adjournment. Section 390.10 of the C.P.L. now requires that a fingerprint report be before the court at the time of sentencing in any case where prints were required to be taken at the time of arrest, namely any felony, misdemeanor, or loitering for prostitution. If prints were taken at the time of arrest, a yellow sheet should be in the court papers. If prints were not taken at the time of arrest, where for example the arrest was for disorderly conduct or harassment, or if the court wants an updated yellow sheet, the court can order a "record and sentence." This means that the case will be adjourned for anywhere from two or three days to two weeks, depending on the availability of the defense attorney, during which time the defendant is fingerprinted and a new yellow sheet is prepared. There is a procedure for getting a yellow sheet the same day by a photo-relay system, but it is very seldom used and the clerks should be consulted before requesting it. Note that the District Attorney can make a motion to the court that a record and sentence be ordered, as can defense counsel. Remember that the question of whether prints are to be taken in a violation case is very important and should be a point of plea bargaining, and remember also that the ordering of a record and sentence means that prints are being taken.

Where a record and sentence (often called an "R and S") has been ordered, the case is adjourned to the same part for sentence. Where there is an agreement made with respect to sentence, but a record and sentence is ordered, the judge will note on the court papers that the matter is to be referred to him for sentencing. On the return date the case is first called in the part where the case was pending and it is then ordered to be sent to the proper judge. Where there has been a conviction after trial and the matter is adjourned for sentencing, the case will appear on the calendar of the part in which the case was tried and the defendant will be sentenced by the judge who happens to be sitting in that part on the sentence date, unless defense counsel has requested at the end of trial that the trial judge sentence the defendant. In making such a request you should argue that the special circumstances of the case are such that justice is better served by the trial judge keeping the case before himself for sentencing. If the trial judge denies your request, but there are facts about the trial that you want the sentencing judge to know about, you can simply visit the trial judge in his chambers and ask him to communicate the special circumstances to the sentencing judge. There is no authority for such a procedure but the court is run by human beings and any arrangements that are physically possible can usually be worked out with some perseverance.

In a case which is tried before the three-judge bench, sentencing can be done by the three trial judges only if the adjournment is short enough (usually within the calendar month) so that those judges are still sitting. In exceptional cases, where the trial bench has disbanded but a special request is made and granted, the trial bench can be reconvened on a particular date for the sole purpose of sentencing. Ordinarily, sentence will be imposed by the three judges who happen to be sitting on the date set for sentencing. Similarly, where a plea is taken before a three-man bench, sentence will be decided by the three judges sitting at the time of sentence. Where a plea is taken in the one-judge calendar part of the three-man bench, the practices described in the preceding paragraph apply.

An "investigation and sentence" requires a longer adjournment, about three weeks if the defendant is in jail and anywhere from four to eight weeks if the defendant is not in jail. Note that Section 45 of the Criminal Court Act requires that the adjournments not exceed 10 days if the defendant is in jail, but, due to the probation department being enormously overworked, this rule is not usually observed. If your client is in jail and if it appears likely that the sentence of the court will be probation or time served (a conditional discharge), you should point out to the court that an adjournment for more than ten days is illegal and you should request that your client be released on bail or parole pending sentence, as authorized by Section 45.

An investigation and sentence (called "I and S" for short) means that a probation report is prepared. A probation officer is assigned to the case, the defendant is interviewed at length, his past activities are summarized for the court, letters are written to his school or past and present employers, military records are obtained, letters are written to any person that is designated as a reference, defendant's parents are interviewed if he is a minor, and he is again fingerprinted and an up-dated yellow sheet is prepared. The detailed report submitted to the court often contains the probation officer's impression of the defendant's attitude; older probation officers look for a re-morseful, repentant attitude, and you should advise your client of this fact. The report does not however contain a specific recommendation. These reports are quite thorough and should not be requested if the defendant's past will not appear favorable under close examination. The defense attorney in a difficult case can be helpful in soliciting letters of recommendation from community workers and officials such as social workers, teachers, former employers, or clergymen. Such letters can be sent directly to the assigned probation officer at the courthouse. Where an investigation and sentence is ordered the case will appear on the adjourned date in the same part where the investigation was ordered, with the same exception to this rule as noted above for records and sentencing.

Of crucial importance is the judge who sentences the defendant. Some judges will sentence anyone with a prior record to a relatively severe jail term while others will send virtually no one to jail who is working or in school. On the other hand, there are many cases in which the sentencing will not vary significantly from judge to judge, such as where the defendant has no prior record or where the case is relatively mild, or where the defendant is in some rehabilitative program. The defense lawyer can to a limited extent choose the judge who is to sentence. This can be done only by having a schedule of judges or, if the adjournment is within the same month, by asking the clerk who will be sitting. Schedules of judges are not available to the public but they can be found in the office of the court reporters (room 320 in New York County) and some lawyers have ob-

135

tained them. Generally speaking a group of judges is assigned to a particular complex of parts, such as the AP1, AP2, AP7 felony parts, or MAP parts, for one or more months and they usually stay in each part for at least several weeks. The clerk's office for each complex has a schedule for that month. Thus if a guilty plea is entered on a particular date and a record and sentence is requested, the matter can be adjourned either for some time later that week, or for one or two weeks, and the adjournment is generally made to suit the attorney's schedule. For an investigation and sentence, the flexibility is even greater, again with the adjournments generally made to suit defense counsel's convenience. The decision on whether to request a record and sentence or even in certain cases an investigation and sentence, should sometimes be made with the schedule of judges in mind.

Probation reports have traditionally been considered by the court to be secret. Section 390.50 of the Criminal Procedure Law directs that the reports be confidential and also the Court of Appeals has held that it was not an abuse of discretion for a court to refuse to permit defense counsel to read the report. Your request to see the report will be denied although it may be wise to make such a request, based on the defendant's right to confront all witnesses and evidence introduced against him at any crucial stage of the proceeding, if you are seeking to insert possible reversible error, which may have to be tested before a level higher than the Court of Appeals. There is also a possibility that this rule will change. Occasionally the judge will call you to the bench and allow you to read the probation report.

Section 390.40 of the C.P.L. gives the defendant the right to submit his own pre-sentence report. If it becomes clear that the probation report conflicts with what you have written or orally stated to be the facts, you can request an adjournment for the purpose of having a conference with the probation officer. Unless the court is inclined to sentence the defendant to probation, your request for an adjournment is likely to be granted since a jail sentence based on an erroneous probation report seems readily attackable on appeal.

At the time of sentencing the court will ask you whether there is any legal cause why sentence should not now be imposed, and upon your answer in the negative, you have the opportunity to make a statement on the defendant's behalf.

The crucial factors considered by the court in sentencing are the defendant's prior record, what he has done and is doing with his life and, of course, the crime itself. Your statement should include whatever you can think of that is favorable about the defendant, including his employment record, his military service record, his previous criminal record (and, where applicable, priors should be explained), whether he lives with his parents (a good sign in the eyes of the criminal court), whether he is married and has children (both generally considered positive factors), the dependants he supports, that the defendant is remorseful, that he has pleaded guilty at an early stage of the proceedings, and any mitigating factors about the case itself. In political cases, depending on the judge and the case, it may be helpful to discuss the politics behind the arrest, what the defendant was fighting for, etc. In heavy political cases, such as a demonstration arrest of weathermen who were breaking windows, it may be advantageous to inform the court, if it is true, that the defendant has severed his ties with the radical organizations since his or her arrest, and now engages in peaceful political activity, or none at all. Where the defendant has a long prior record but has not been in trouble for several years, that fact should be pointed out to the court. Parents, husbands or wives and children should appear in court and stand behind the guard rail at the time of sentencing and their presence should be pointed out to the court.

The sentence actually imposed depends very much on the case, the defendant's background, and the judge, but there are certain general guidelines that can be given. Persons convicted of violations rarely receive jail sentences even where they have pleaded guilty to the violation in satisfaction of misdemeanor charges (although there are a few judges who consistently give the maximum sentence to anyone who loses a trial of a violation and you should avoid a trial before these judges). First offenders in all but the most serious cases generally do not receive jail sentences, with the sentence being probation for youths and young adults, and a conditional discharge or a fine for adults or where the offense is mild. An exception is in heavy political cases, such as the Columbia bust in Spring, 1968, where some judges wanted to make examples out of the particular defendants and sentenced first offenders to 15 days in a jail on a plea to a violation. A sentence of probation is generally given only once; that is, if a person was convicted of being a youthful offender at age 18 and successfully completed two years of probation, and he is again convicted at age 21, he will generally not receive another sentence of probation. He may, however, be given a conditional discharge if he is doing well and the crime is not too serious. A conviction of another crime while a defendant is on probation for a previous conviction makes a jail sentence more likely, although frequently if the defendant is doing something which the courts view as constructive, the court will allow the defendant to continue on probation. Once a person has served jail sentences in the past, he is then very likely to receive a jail sentence on subsequent convictions, especially if there are short time intervals between convictions. If the crimes are similar in gravity then each jail sentence is likely to be longer than the last, all other factors being equal. Sentences of probation, reformatory, or in excess of 90 days in prison cannot be imposed unless a pre-sentence report has been prepared. An investigation and sentence may of course be ordered in any other case.

Sentences that may be imposed on youths, aged 16 to 21, are in a complicated and I think partially illegal state of affairs. Article 75 of the Penal Law and § 720.55 of the C.P.L. describe the various sentences. To sum them up, upon a felony conviction in Supreme Court, whether or not defendant was given Y.O. treatment, the jail sentence can be either the same sentence that could be given to an adult, or a sentence to the state reformatory of up to 4 years (in practice they are generally paroled after about 18–22 months in), or a sentence to the city reformatory of up to 3 years (eligible for parole after 9 months). In misdemeanor cases where Y.O. was granted, the jail sentence can only be in the range of time that an adult could be sentenced to. In non-Y.O. misdemeanor cases against youths 16 to 21, however, the Criminal Court can actually impose a 0–4 year state reformatory or 0–3 year city reformatory sentence, despite the fact that an adult could not get such a severe sentence. Amazingly, these sentences were upheld in *Meltsner v. Folleter*, 32 A.D. 2d 389, 302 N.Y.S. 2d 624 (2d Dept. 1969), upon the preposterous rationale that the rehabilitation supposedly given to youths justifies a longer sentence.

Chapter 13

APPEALS

Appeals in criminal cases can generally be taken only from judgments of conviction. An exception to this rule are cases where suits are brought either in Supreme or Federal court to enjoin the continued prosecution of a case, usually on some constitutional ground. An example of such a case is *Hogan v. Rosenberg*, 24 N.Y. 2d 207 (1969), in which Judge Jack Rosenberg granted a defense motion for a jury trial in a misdemeanor case and the District Attorney's office brought an Article 78 proceeding against the judges of the Criminal Court to enjoin them from proceeding by jury trial. Note that judgment is deemed to be entered at the time of sentencing, not conviction.

All that will be described in this chapter is how to initiate an appeal and how to get your client out of jail pending the appeal. The manner of preparing records for appeals is set forth in the rules of the various courts. Note that an appeal from a judgment of the Criminal Court is to the Appellate Term of the Supreme Court, while an appeal from the Supreme Court is to the Appellate Division.

If you intend to appeal, and you expect your client to be given a jail sentence, then all the papers described in this chapter should be prepared prior to the date of sentencing. Getting your client out of jail pending appeal is a two-step process: (1) Filing the notice of appeal, and (2) obtaining a certificate of reasonable doubt, which is a court order allowing the defendant to be released on bail pending appeal, on the ground that there is a reasonable doubt about the validity of the judgment.

Filing the notice of appeal is very easy. Simply prepare an original and three copies of a notice of appeal (see appendix

139

page 165), bring all copies to the clerk's office of the District Attorney's office (7th floor of 155 Leonard Street in New York County), serve one copy on the clerk and have him mark all others "copy received" with the date and time, and then serve the original and one copy on the clerk of the Appellate Term (Room 238 of the Criminal Court of New York County). The remaining copy is for your file.

The procedure for obtaining a certificate of reasonable doubt from the Supreme Court is somewhat more complicated. Three documents must be prepared: a notice of motion for a certificate of reasonable doubt, an order granting the certificate of reasonable doubt and fixing bail, and an affidavit in support of the motion for the certificate. See the appendix pages 166 through 170. The notice of motion and order are forms and can be copied with appropriate changes. The affidavit in support of the motion should contain all the grounds you can think of that can persuade the court that there is a reasonable doubt about the validity of the conviction. Your affidavit may sound stronger if you have objected to some of the procedures of the criminal court, even where those procedures may not be particularly relevant to your case. For example, if you feel there may be an appeal of a case in which a defendant was granted youthful offender treatment, you should request a preliminary hearing after Y.O. is granted (see chapter 8), and, after your request is denied, state for the record that you "respectfully take exception to the court's ruling."

After you have served the Notice of Appeal, bring all the papers in support of your application for a certificate of reasonable doubt, together with any favorable transcripts you might have, to one of the attorneys in the Appeals Bureau of the District Attorney's office. Your purpose is to get him to consent to the issuance of the certificate of reasonable doubt and to agree to as low a bail as possible. Tell him about the issues you wish to appeal, why you think they are valid, about the case itself if it is light enough, and give him the bail facts about the defendant. Before consenting he may wish to discuss the matter with the assistant district attorney who tried the case, but, if the sentence is four months or less and the case raises some issues that are colorably appealable, he will usually consent. If he consents and you are able to agree on a bail, he will note his consent directly on your papers and all you have to do is bring them to part 30 of the Supreme Court (the motion part) for the judge's signature. The judge will see that the District Attorney has consented and he will readily sign the papers. If the D.A. in the Appeals Bureau does not consent, then the matter must be argued before the judge in Part 30. The procedure for setting this up is to bring all your papers to the clerk of Part 30 (who sits in the courtroom) and ask him to add your case to the motion calendar. If it is late he may refuse and you may have to argue it the next day. Also you should try to bring the D.A. from the Appeals Bureau with you to Part 30 so that you can argue the motion, and hopefully get a favorable disposition, on the spot. Otherwise the assistant in Part 30 will probably ask for an adjournment so that a D.A. familiar with the case can be gotten into court. Like any other motion, copies must be served on the District Attorney's office, although § 460.50 of the C.P.L. states only that the notice be reasonable.

After the judge has signed the original order granting the certificate of reasonable doubt and fixing bail (which is often set at $1), you must conform the copies and have the judge's stamp placed on them. You must then have a copy certified (which costs $1) in the office of the general clerk of the Supreme Court (room 141 of 60 Centre Street in New York County). Bring the certified copy together with the bail to whichever jail the defendant is being held in and, presto, your client will be released.

APPENDIX — FORMS

1. Motion for free transcript
2. Motion for Bill of Particulars
3. Motion for discovery
4. Motion for disclosure of results of electronic surveillance
5. Motion for disclosure of written documents
6. Motion to suppress evidence on grounds of illegal search
7. Motion to controvert search warrant
8. Motion to suppress identification
9. Motion to suppress statements
10. Writ and petition for writ of habeas corpus
11. Judicial subpoena duces tecum
12. Notice of appeal
13.a Notice of motion for certificate of reasonable doubt
13.b Affidavit in support of certificate of reasonable doubt
13.c Order granting certificate of reasonable doubt and admitting defendant to bail
14. Motion for new trial
15. Motion to inspect grand jury minutes and dismiss indictment (or information).

Form 1 — MOTION FOR
   FREE TRANSCRIPT

At a Trial Term, Part   of
the Criminal Court of the
City of New York, held in
and for the County of New
York, on the   day of
1969.

PRESENT:

Hon. _____

THE PEOPLE OF THE STATE OF NEW YORK
                    —against—

_____ Defendant

DOCKET NO.

Order granting
defendant free
transcript

The defendant   by his attorney,
                having applied by motion for a transcript of a pre-
liminary hearing held in the Criminal Court on June 12, 1969, in Part 1B-2
thereof, before Hon.   , Justice, it is hereby
   ORDERED that   , an official court reporter of the
Criminal Court of the City of New York, County of New York, furnish
counsel for defendant a free copy of the stenographer's minutes of the
above proceeding, in accordance with Section 302 of the Judiciary Law,
and that the said court reporter be compensated therefor pursuant to
subdivision 2 of said section, said transcript being required by the defendant at the trial of the above-captioned case now pending in this court.

ENTER:

J.C.C.

CAPTION: REQUEST FOR TRANSCRIPT
         OF PRELIMINARY HEARING
         WITHOUT PAYMENT OF COST
         OR FEES

DOCKET NO.

STATE OF NEW YORK)
COUNTY OF NEW YORK)   ss.

                    being duly sworn, deposes and says:
   1. I am the defendant in the above-entitled action and I make this
affidavit in support of the annexed motion for a transcript of the preliminary hearing without payment of cost or fees.
   2. A preliminary hearing was held and testimony recorded in the
above-entitled action in Part 1B-2 of the Criminal Court before Hon.
                on   19   .

143

3. I am presently unable to pay the cost of the minutes of that proceeding. I am disabled due to psychiatric illness and am presently supported by welfare. I am presently unemployed, I have no phone, no bank account, no money except for a few dollars, no property, and no securities.

4. I am presently being represented by counsel who is serving without fee because of my indigence.

5. I have made no prior application for this transcript.

WHEREFORE, your deponent respectfully requests that he be provided with the transcript of his preliminary hearing without payment of costs or fees.

Sworn to before me this
    day of   , 1969.

SUPREME COURT OF THE STATE OF NEW YORK
COUNTY OF NEW YORK

THE PEOPLE OF THE STATE OF NEW YORK Indictment No.
      —against—

_____ Defendant   NOTICE OF MO-
TION FOR BILL
OF PARTICU-
LARS

SIR:

    PLEASE TAKE NOTICE that upon the annexed affidavit of
    , dated   , 19 , the undersigned will move the
Supreme Court, County of New York, Part 30, on the   day of
    , 19 , at 10 o'clock in the forenoon of that day, or as soon
thereafter as counsel can be heard, for an order requiring the District
Attorney of the County of New York to furnish to the defendant or his
counsel within a time to be fixed in said order a bill of particulars which
shall set forth:

    1. As to each and every count of the indictment the acts that the
defendant   is alleged to have directly committed and those acts of
the other named defendants which the defendant is alleged to have aided
or abetted in their commission and those acts which the defendant
      is alleged to have counseled, commanded, induced or procured
another of the named defendants to directly commit.

    2. As to each and every count of the indictment, if the defendant
      is not alleged to have directly committed those acts alleged in
such counts, the name of the other named defendants alleged to have
directly committed such acts, and for such other and proper relief as to
this court may seem just and proper.

CAPTION —
STATE OF NEW YORK)
COUNTY OF NEW YORK) ss.:

                    , being an attorney at law associated
with   , attorney of record for the defendant herein, affirms under penalties of perjury:

    1. I am the attorney for   , one of the defendants herein, who
is charged in this indictment with the crimes of robbery, burglary, assault,
rape and sodomy.

2. Your deponent believes that if the defendant ___ is to be prepared to meet the charges against him it is necessary that he be informed as to what acts it is alleged that he directly committed, what acts he is alleged to have aided or abetted the other named defendants, what acts it is alleged that he counselled or induced another of the named defendants to commit directly, and, if it is alleged that he aided, abetted, counselled, or induced certain acts, which of the named defendants directly committed those acts.

3. Your deponent further believes that without such particulars the defendant, ___ , cannot safely proceed to trial in this action as your deponent will not be able to properly prepare his case due to the large number of counts in the indictment and the fact that from the indictment there is no way of knowing which of the four defendants committed the act alleged in each count. I believe that such information is within the control and knowledge of the District Attorney of the County of New York and that same may not be obtained from any other source.

WHEREFORE, I respectfully ask that an order be made herein directing the District Attorney of the County of New York to furnish counsel for defendant a bill of particulars in accordance with the demands set forth in the annexed notice of motion.

Dated: New York, New York
        , 19

Form 3 — MOTION FOR DISCOVERY
CAPTION — NOTICE OF MOTION FOR DISCOVERY

SIRS:

PLEASE TAKE NOTICE, that upon the annexed affirmation of
, duly affirmed on the   day of
, 19   , and upon the indictment herein, the undersigned will
move this Court at Part 30 thereof, at the Courthouse located at 100
Centre Street, City, County and State of New York, on the   day
of   , 19   , at 10:00 A.M. or as soon thereafter as counsel can
be heard, for an Order:

1. Permitting defendant to obtain the names and whereabouts of all
persons who were arrested with the defendant herein, regardless of
whether the District Attorney intends to have them testify either at the
trial of or at the trial of the defendant herein; and

2. Permitting defendant to obtain the names and whereabouts of all
persons who acted as agents for law enforcement agencies or who supplied
information to law enforcement agencies, and who at any time witnessed
X in possession of the various weapons enumerated in indictment No.
, or who has any evidence relating to X's purchase, ownership,
use of, defacement of, or possession of said weapons, regardless of whether
the District Attorney intends to have them testify either at the trial of X
or at the trial of the defendant herein; and

3. Ordering that the information requested in paragraph 1 and 2 above
be turned over to defendant forthwith on the ground that the information
is vital to defendant's preparation for trial and that the information is
rapidly becoming stale;

And for such other and further relief as to the court may seem just and
proper under the circumstances.

CAPTION —   AFFIRMATION IN SUPPORT OF
             MOTION FOR DISCOVERY

, an attorney-at-law duly licensed to practice in the
Courts of the State of New York, affirms the following under the penalty
of perjury:

1. I am the attorney for the above-named defendant and I make this
affirmation in support of the annexed Motion for Discovery.

2. Defendant,   was   arrested   on
, 19   , while in an apartment with one X. X is one of a
number of defendants named in indictment No.   and he is
presently awaiting trial on charges of conspiracy to commit murder and
various other substantive crimes. Indictment No.   alleges that X

147

conspired from on or about to on or about
, with others named in that indictment.

3. On information and belief, the government intends to introduce evidence of meetings which took place at which agreements between the persons named in indictment No. were allegedly made.

4. On information and belief, the government intends to introduce evidence alleging that the various items found in the apartment occupied by X and the defendant herein were to be used in furtherance of the conspiracy.

5. A subsequent indictment has been returned against X alleging that he possessed the very same items which the defendant herein is accused of possessing.

6. It is not alleged that defendant, , had any connection with the conspiracy alleged in indictment No.

7. On information and belief, the government knows the names of persons who were acting as agents of law enforcement agencies and who have knowledge of the purchasing, obtaining, defacing, use of, or possession of the above mentioned weapons by X.

8. Clearly evidence of this character is exculpatory to defendant herein and must be furnished to the accused. *Brady v. Maryland*, 373 U.S. 83 (1963).

9. In this case, due process requires that the requested information be given to the defendant immediately. As Judge Frankel said in *United States v. Gleason.* 265 F. Supp. 880 (S.D.N.Y. 1967), there should be no "blanket postponing to the trial all disclosures of the type in question", since "information may come too late for effective preparation if it is not delivered until the case is on trial." On information and belief there are numerous witnesses whose names must be given to defendant and it will be impossible for defendant and counsel to interview these witnesses and prepare for trial if these names are given to defendant only when the case is on trial.

10. It should not be left to the discretion of the prosecution to determine what evidence may be relevant or useful to the defendant in proving her innocence. As Judge Frankel pointed out in *United States v. Gleason, supra,* such an approach would leave with the more powerful adversary "a critical period of unilateral control that must at least sometimes exact an unacceptable toll of unfair convictions." "The determination of what may be useful to the defense can properly and effectively be made only by an advocate." *Dennis v. United States,* 384 U.S. 855, 875, (1966).

11. No prior application has been made for the relief requested herein.

WHEREFORE, your deponent respectfully requests that the annexed Motion for Discovery be granted in all respects, and that the court grant such other and further relief as it may deem just and proper under the circumstances.

148

Form 4 — MOTION FOR DISCLOSURE OF RESULTS OF ELEC-TRONIC SURVEILLANCE
CAPTION: NOTICE OF MOTION FOR DISCLOSURE OF RESULTS OF SURVEILLANCE.

SIRS:

PLEASE TAKE NOTICE that upon the annexed affirmation of and upon all proceedings heretofore had herein, the undersigned will move this Court, in Part 30 thereof, held at 100 Centre Street, New York, New York, on the   day of   , 19   , at 10:00 a.m. or as soon thereafter as counsel can be heard, for an order directing the People of the State of New York to disclose to defendants, pursuant to the Fourth and Fourteenth Amendment of the U.S. Constitution:

1. Any and all logs, records and memoranda resulting from electronic surveillance of conversations by or with defendant herein, concerning the ownership, possession or use of various weapons enumerated in Indictment No.   by either the defendant herein or by X.

2. Any and all logs, records and memoranda resulting from electronic surveillance of conversations concerning the ownership, possession, or use of various weapons enumerated in Indictment No.   by anyone in the apartment in which the defendant herein was arrested.

3. Any and all logs, records and memoranda resulting from electronic surveillance of conversations concerning the lease, tenancy or occupancy of the apartment in which the defendant herein was arrested.

4. Any and all logs, records and memoranda resulting from electronic surveillance of conversations which took place in the apartment in which defendant herein was arrested by any persons at any time prior to defendant's arrest.

5. Any and all logs, records and memoranda of conversations conversations concerning the alleged conspiracy and substantive crimes of which X is accused in Indictment No.

These requests seek not only surveillance which in the exercise of due diligence may become known; they seek surveillance conducted by any agency of the local, state, or federal government and continuing disclosure of same.

Defendant further moves for an evidentiary hearing prior to trial to determine whether the District Attorney has turned over all applicable records of electronic surveillance.

The grounds for this motion are more particularly set forth in accompanying affirmation of counsel.

Dated: New York, New York

149

, 19   Yours, etc.
                              Name, address and phone of attorney
To: District Attorney   for defendant
      New York County
      Clerk, Supreme Court
      New York County

CAPTION—AFFIRMATION IN SUPPORT OF MOTION FOR DIS-
CLOSURE OF RESULTS OF SURVEILLANCE

STATE OF NEW YORK)
COUNTY OF NEW YORK) ss.:
                            , an attorney-at-law duly licensed to
practice in the courts of the State of New York, duly affirms the following
under penalty of perjury.

1. I am the attorney for the above-named defendant and I make this
affirmation in support of the annexed motion for disclosure of results of
electronic surveillance.

2. On information and belief, electronic surveillance was conducted in
the apartment in which the defendant and X were arrested, and was directed at the defendant herein, X, and others. On further information and
belief, electronic surveillance directed against X was conducted at other
locations.

3. Defendant was arrested on   , 19   , while present in
an apartment with X. X is one of a number of defendants named in
Indictment No.   and is presently awaiting trial on charges of
conspiracy to commit murder and various substantive crimes. Indictment
No.   alleges that X conspired with others from on or about
                      , to on or about

4. On information and belief, a subsequent indictment has been returned against X which alleges that he possessed the very same weapons
that defendant herein is accused of possessing in Indictment No.
      . The defendant herein is not named in the conspiracy indict-
ment.

5. Under these circumstances, it is clear that any statements made by
anyone concerning the ownership, possession or use of weapons by anyone
in the apartment in which defendant herein was arrested, or by X in or out
of the apartment in question, might be exculpatory to the defendant
herein. Furthermore, any conversations implicating X in the conspiracy or
in substantive crimes could be exculpatory to the defendant herein. As
such, they must be disclosed to defendant upon demand. *Brady v. Maryland*, 373 U.S. 83 (1963).

6. On information and belief, the contraband was allegedly found by the police somewhere in the apartment occupied by X and the defendant herein, not on the person of either of them. Therefore, any statements made by anyone concerning the lease, tenancy or occupancy of the apartment in question could be exculpatory to defendant herein. Furthermore, the records of all conversations in the apartment in question could be exculpatory to defendant since they could show that he was not in the apartment for extended periods of time, which in itself shows a lesser degree of contact with the apartment, and would therefore be exculpatory.

7. In this case due process requires that the requested material be given to defendant immediately. As Judge Frankel said in *United States v. Gleason*, 265 F. Supp. 880 (S.D. N.Y.), there should be no "blanket postponint to trial all disclosures of the type in question", since "information may come too late for effective preparation if it is not delivered until the case is on trial." The information requested may lead the defendant to numerous witnesses and it will be impossible for defendant and counsel to locate and interview these witnesses and prepare for trial if the names are given to defendant only at the commencement of the trial.

8. It should not be left to the discretion of the prosecution to determine what evidence may be relevant or useful to the defendant in proving innocence. As Judge Frankel pointed out in *United States v. Gleason*, *supra*, such an approach would leave with the more powerful of the adversary "a critical period of unilateral control that must at least sometimes exact an unacceptable toll of unfair convictions." "The determination of what may be useful to the defense can properly and effectively be made only by an advocate. *Dennis v. United States*, 384 U.S. 855, 875 (1966).

9. No prior application has been made for the relief requested herein.

WHEREFORE, your deponent respectfully requests that the annexed motion for disclosure of results of electronic surveillance be granted in all respects, and that the court grant such other and further relief as to the court may seem just and proper under the circumstances.

CAPTION—NOTICE OF MOTION FOR DISCLOSURE OF WRITTEN DOCUMENTS

SIRS:

PLEASE TAKE NOTICE that on the annexed affidavits of and , the defendant will move this Court, in Part 2B thereof at 100 Centre Street, on the day of , 19 , at 9:30 o'clock in the forenoon, or as soon thereafter as counsel can be heard, for an order directing the District Attorney to produce for the inspection of defendant's attorney at or before the trial of this action:

1. All writings, records, memoranda or directives now in the custody of the New York City Police Department concerning the defendant.

2. All writings, records, memoranda or directives of the Chief of Detectives Special Unit (CDSU) of the Police Department, or any officer or agent thereof concerning the defendant herein and anyone allegedly acting in concert with him:

(a) Made at any time, and

(b) Made during the month immediately preceding , 19 , the date of the arrest at issue here.

3. All writings, records, memoranda or directives now in the custody of the New York City Police Department, its agents, servants or employees, concerning the alleged co-conspirator herein,

4. All writings, records, memoranda or directives of the CDSU of the Police Department, or any officer of agent thereof, concerning the said alleged co-conspirator,

(a) Made at any time, and

(b) Made during the month immediately preceding , 19 ,

5. All writings, records, memoranda or directives prepared by or under the direction of Detective , CDSU, the arresting officer herein, concerning:

(a) Defendant , and anyone allegedly acting in concert with him, and

(b) Alleged co-conspirator.

and for such other and further relief as to the Court may seem just and proper.

Dated: New York, New York
, 19

CAPTION—AFFIRMATION OF ATTORNEY IN SUPPORT OF MOTION FOR DISCLOSURE OF WRITTEN DOCUMENTS.

, affirms, under the penalties of perjury:

1. I am a member of the Bar of this Court, with offices at , and I am counsel for the defendant herein. The defendant is accused of conspiracy by, in effect, whispering inflammatory phrases to one , which were supposed to have been repeated to a crowd on East Sixth Street. The arresting officer claims that he overheard the words.

2. This affidavit is made in support of the defendant's motion to obtain certain records of the Police Department concerning its investigation of the defendant.

3. The officer who made the arrest in this case is in the Chief of Detectives Special Unit, a special detachment of detectives, one of the duties of which, on information and belief, is to investigate alleged troublemakers. Agents of the CDSU, including the arresting officer herein, had been following the defendant and his friends about for at least two days. The annexed affidavit of the defendant explains the circumstances fully and in fact the officer himself said at the preliminary hearing that "the night before we drank beer together" (minutes of hearing, p. 15, copy annexed hereto).

The defense contends that officers of the CDSU including the arresting detective were assigned to pursue the defendant and his friends including Mr. , and that these officers resolved to make an arrest at all costs. The course of conduct of the officer, as shown by the annexed affidavit as well as the preliminary hearing, lends credibility to these contentions. It is quite apparent from the course of conduct of the officers that they did not merely choose the defendant by accident, but pursuant to a plan. The revelation of that plan is of the essence of the defense in this case, and it is for that reason that the present motion is made. The arrest made in this case was the culmination of several days of work, and probably of more. The reports of that work are essential to put the present case in its proper context, and to defend the accused. On information and belief these reports must exist. Officers of the CDSU did not by sheer accident begin to trail the defendant and his friends about and strike up conversations with them, they did not continue the practice for days, without some preconceived plan, followed by progress reports, and possibly by directives from above. Under the circumstances, it is essential that these reports be made available to the defendant.

5. The reports made by the arresting officer and others of the CDSU are essential to show the bias of the prosecution witnesses, and to attack

their credibility. Moreover, they no doubt contain reports precisely of the conversations and activities to which the witness or witnesses will testify at the trial. They will contain prior statements of witnesses. From every point of view, they are essential tools of cross-examination as well as essential to the proof of the case for the defense. Without these reports, the defendant cannot get due process of law, an adequate defense, or a fair trial.

WHEREFORE, it is respectfully submitted that the relief prayed for in this motion should be granted.

CAPTION—AFFIDAVIT OF DEFENDANT IN SUPPORT OF MOTION FOR DISCLOSURE.

_____, being duly sworn, deposes and says:

1. On _____, 19___, at about 6:00 P.M. I attended a peaceable rally at 116th Street and Amsterdam Avenue. I there met and conversed with a Negro man wearing a pendant around his neck. I later saw him patrolling the campus, and concluded that he was a policeman. I do not know his name.

2. The following evening, I was with a group of friends at Ninth Street and Second Avenue. I saw the same man I had seen the night before, standing south of us on Second Avenue, in the company of Det. X, the arresting officer in this case, Det. Y, another policeman, and still another man. I walked west on Ninth Street in the company of _____, Det. X and the first man followed us while the other officers followed our friends. Det. X and the other man stopped us, asked us what we were doing and asked who was paying. We walked away, and the two officers pursued us wherever we went. Some time later, Mr. _____ and I bought beer and drank it sitting on some benches at Houston Street. The original officer claimed that he and Det. X were "Five Percenters" and attempted to engage us in conversation. I asked them when they went "off shift," meaning to imply that they were policemen.

3. At about 9:30 on _____, 19___, the following day, I was on East Sixth Street, where a community demonstration was in progress. I was with _____ and _____, After an arrest was made, I left the scene in the company of Dets. X and Y and about 10 others were following us. _____ went into a storefront, where I later heard he was arrested.

4. Later in the evening, I was on St. Marks Place. Dets. X and Y came up to me, placed me under arrest and took me to the Seventh Precinct.

5. When I arrived in the precinct, _____ was already there in custody, though we were separated. I was interviewed by a

sergeant, who made a telephone call, in which he said first, "Do you recognize my voice?" followed by, "I've only got one of them and the Spanish guy."

Sworn to before me this
   day of   , 1970

Defendant

Form 6 — MOTION TO SUPPRESS EVIDENCE ON GROUNDS OF ILLEGAL SEARCH

CRIMINAL COURT OF THE CITY OF NEW YORK
COUNTY OF NEW YORK

PEOPLE OF THE STATE OF NEW YORK —against— _____ Defendant	NOTICE OF MOTION TO SUPPRESS EVIDENCE ON GROUNDS OF ILLEGAL SEARCH Doc.No.:

SIR:

PLEASE TAKE NOTICE, that upon the annexed affidavit of
, dated   , 1969, the undersigned
will move the Criminal Court, County of New York, 100 Centre Street,
New York, New York, Part 1-B, on the   day of   , 19,   at
9:30 A.M., or as soon thereafter as counsel can be heard for an order
suppressing evidence obtained by an illegal search and seizure, and for such
other and further relief as to the court may seem just and proper under the
circumstances.

CAPTION—AFFIDAVIT IN SUPPORT OF MOTION TO SUPPRESS
STATE OF NEW YORK)
COUNTY OF NEW YORK— ss.:

, being duly sworn, deposes and says:

1. I am the defendant in the above designated case and I make this
affidavit in support of a motion to suppress various items which I believe
the prosecutor intends to introduce as evidence against me at my trial in
the Criminal Court.

2. On the   day of   , 1969, at approximately 1:00 A.M. I
was walking on Rutgers Street, in the City, County and State of New
York.

3. At that time the arresting officer and another officer, both members
of the New York City Police Department, stopped me, searched my person
and searched a box which I was carrying, and the arresting officer alleges
that he found a stolen telephone in said box.

4. The arresting officer showed me no search warrant. I did not consent to the search, and I believe that he did not have probable cause to
believe that a crime was being committed before he searched my person.

5. The aforesaid search and seizure was a violation of my rights under
the Fourth and Fourteenth Amendments to the U.S. Constitution.

WHEREFORE, I respectfully request that an order be made and entered suppressing the use of the aforementioned items in my trial in this
case, and for such other and further relief as to this Court may seem just
and proper under the circumstances.

Sworn to before me this
        day of   , 1969.

Form 7 — MOTION TO CONTROVERT SEARCH WARRANT
CAPTION — NOTICE OF MOTION TO CONTROVERT SEARCH WARRANT

SIRS:

PLEASE TAKE NOTICE that upon the annexed affidavit of , Esq., attorney for defendant, and upon all prior proceedings herein, the undersigned will move this court on the day of , 1970, at 9:30 A.M. or as soon thereafter as counsel can be heard, at the Courthouse located at 100 Centre Street, New York, New York, Part 1B1 thereof, for an order controverting and vacating the search warrant herein, described more fully in the affirmation in support of this motion, and suppressing the use of evidence discovered as a result of the use of that search warrant, and for such other and further relief as to this court may seem just and proper under the circumstances.

Yours, etc.
Attorney for defendant

TO: Clerk: Criminal Court: Part 1B1
District Attorney: New York County

CAPTION—AFFIRMATION IN SUPPORT OF MOTION TO CONTROVERT SEARCH WARRANT
STATE OF NEW YORK)
COUNTY OF NEW YORK)

, an attorney at law duly licensed to practice in the Courts of the State of New York, affirms the following under penalty of perjury:

1. I am the attorney for the defendant herein and I make this affirmation in support of the annexed motion to controvert the search warrant, described below, and to suppress the evidence obtained through the use of said search warrant.

2. On the day of , 1970, a search warrant was issued by Judge , in the Supreme Court, New York County, directing the Police Department to search Apt. , in , New York, N.Y. The application for the warrant was supported by an affidavit of Det. dated . Copies of the warrant, application and affidavit are annexed hereto and designated defendant's exhibits A, B, and C, respectively.

157

3. As a result of the issuance, execution and return of said warrant, the defendant was arrested and charged with possession of dangerous drugs with intent to sell, a felony, and said charges have since been reduced to possession of a dangerous drug as a misdemeanor on   , 1970, by order of Judge   . A preliminary hearing was held in Part 1B1 on   before Judge

4. The affidavit by Det.   of the Narcotics Bureau is defective for several reasons:

(a) Not sufficient information was given to the issuing judge which shows that the alleged informer was reliable. The mere recital of two cases in which information from said informer led to 2 arrests, without mention of convictions, is, without more, clearly insufficient.

(b) The information alleged to have been supplied by the informer was insufficient to base a finding of probable cause that a crime was being committed in the defendant's apartment. The informer's statements that numerous known drug addicts were seen entering the house in which the defendant resides cannot form the basis for the issuance of a warrant. The defendant lives in a house with two separate apartments in it and a statement that addicts were entering the house, without designating the apartment, cannot support a finding of probable cause that a crime was being committed in defendant's apartment.

(c) The "no knock" provision in the warrant was not supported by any specific evidence, only the most conclusory generalities.

(d) The dates that Det.   allegedly received his information are not given and, on information and belief, said information was stale at the time the warrant was applied for.

WHEREFORE, your deponent respectfully requests that an order be made and entered controverting and vacating the above-mentioned search warrant and suppressing the evidence discovered by its use, and for such other and further relief as to this court may seem just and proper under the circumstances.

DATED: New York, N.Y.
            , 1970

FORM 8 — MOTION TO SUPPRESS IDENTIFICATION

Adapt Form 6 for a NOTICE OF MOTION TO SUPPRESS IDENTIFICATION

CAPTION—AFFIDAVIT IN SUPPORT OF MOTION TO SUPPRESS IDENTIFICATION

STATE OF NEW YORK) ss.:
COUNTY OF NEW YORK)

                    , being duly sworn, deposes and says:

I am the defendant in the above-entitled action. That on or about   1969, I was arrested by Patrolman   of the Housing Authority Police. As a result of that arrest I am now being charged with burglary and other crimes.

That subsequent to my arrest on   , 1969, I was viewed by Mr.   , a complainant in the above-entitled action,   for purposes of identification. I did not have counsel present, nor was I advised of my right to have counsel present, at the time of this encounter. I was viewed alone and without a lineup. My arrest occured several days after the alleged crime and the police had ample opportunity to organize a line-up.

Any evidence of identification thereby obtained was the result of this unconstitutional identification procedure.

The complainant testified at the preliminary hearing held on   in Part 1B2 of the Criminal Court before Hon.   , that he only viewed the alleged burglar for an instant, as the burglar was climbing out a window. Therefore all subsequent identifications are tainted by the first unconstitutional one, including all in-court identifications, and all identification evidence herein should be suppressed.

No prior application has been made for the relief requested.

WHEREFORE your deponent prays that an order be made and entered suppressing all identification evidence herein, and for such other and further relief as to the court may seem just and proper under the circumstances.

                                 Defendant

Sworn to before me this
    day of   , 1969.

159

FORM 9 — MOTION TO SUPPRESS STATEMENTS
Adapt Form 6 for a NOTICE OF MOTION TO SUPPRESS STATEMENTS
CAPTION—AFFIDAVIT IN SUPPORT OF MOTION TO SUPPRESS
STATEMENTS
STATE OF NEW YORK)
COUNTY OF NEW YORK) ss.:

                                  , being duly sworn, deposes and says:

1. I am the defendant herein and I make this affidavit in support of the annexed motion to suppress statements allegedly made by me at the time of my arrest.

2. A preliminary hearing was held in this case on   ,
1970, before Judge   , in Part 1B2 of this Court.

3. At the preliminary hearing the police officer testified that he was directed to go to my home in response to a call from my mother that she found marijuana in her son's coat. The officer testified that he went to the apartment, took the alleged contraband out of a coat, found it to be apparently marijuana, and then waited for me to come home. The officer testified that my mother told him the coat was mine (I have two brothers) and that when I came home the officer asked me if the coat was mine. He testified that I answered affirmatively. A photostatic copy of the minutes of the preliminary hearing are attached.

4. I was never advised of my rights as required by *Miranda v. Arizona*, 384 U.S. 436 (1966), and I was clearly the focus of the investigation at the time I was questioned.

WHEREFORE, I respectfully request that an order be made and entered suppressing the use as evidence statements allegedly made by me at the time of my arrest.

FORM 10 — WRIT AND PETITION FOR WRIT OF HABEAS CORPUS

SUPREME COURT OF THE STATE OF NEW YORK
COUNTY OF THE BRONX
PEOPLE OF THE STATE OF NEW YORK
EX REL
ON BEHALF OF
         —against—
ARTHUR J. SINGERMAN, WARDEN OF BRONX
HOUSE OF DETENTION FOR MEN,
               Defendant

To: ARTHUR J. SINGERMAN, Warden of the Bronx House of Detention for Men.

Greeting:

   WE COMMAND YOU, that you have and produce the body of the said by you imprisoned and detained, as it is said, together with your full return to this writ, and the time and cause of such imprisonment and detention by whatsoever name the said person shall be called or charged before Hon.   one of the Justices of the Supreme Court of the State of New York, county of The Bronx at Part I, 851 Grand Concourse, Bronx, New York in the courthouse thereof on the   day of   , 19   at 10:00 A.M. to do and receive what shall then and there be considered concerning the said person and have you then and there this writ.

WITNESS, Hon.   one of the Justices of our said Court, the   day of   , 1970

                     Clerk

           Name and address of attorney

The within writ is hereby allowed this   day of   , 19

                   J.S.C.

CAPTION — PETITION FOR WRIT OF HABEAS CORPUS

To the Honorable Supreme Court of the State of New York, County of The Bronx.

The Petition of   , by his attorney,   , respectfully shows:

1. I am an attorney admitted to the Bar of this Court with office at   , City, County and State of New York, and I am counsel to   , the defendant herein.

2.   is detained at the Bronx House of Detention for Men, and the officer by whom he is detained is   , Warden of the said House of Detention.

3. The cause or pretense for the detention of   is that he is charged in the Criminal Court, Bronx County, with the crimes of felonious assault, possession of a dangerous weapon, resisting arrest, and the violation of disorderly conduct. He is alleged to have assaulted a police officer on   at   ,   and a copy of the charges is attached as Exhibit A. No preliminary hearing has been held.

4.   is held by virtue of mandates of the Criminal Court setting his bail at $. He has been so detained since   , and two applications for reduction of bail have been made in Criminal Court, both of which have been denied.

5. This bail of   is excessive and arbitrary, and the incarceration of   ,   by reason of such bail terms is in violation of his rights under the New York State Constitution, Article I, Section 5 and the United States Constitution, Amendments 8 and 14.

6. The relator has been detained since   , 19   , without a preliminary hearing, on information and belief because the prosecutor proposed to bring this case before the Grand Jury and foreclose a hearing. At the last adjourned day of his case in Criminal Court,   , , 19   , the prosecutor said that he was not ready, although the arresting officer, who is the complaining witness, was present and able to testify. The relator is being held while the People seek to circumvent CCP §190.

7. Bail may only be used to insure the appearance of the defendant and not for detention. In this case, the character, background and circumstances of relator are such that there is no difficulty in insuring his appearance if he is released. He is twenty-one years old and lives with his mother and family at

At the time of his arrest, he was in the U.S. Army. He had just completed thirteen months of duty, including a tour in Viet Nam, on information and belief under honorable conditions, and he was on leave. I have spoken to Capt.   of the Judge Advocate General's office in Ft. Wadsworth and he has informed me that the Army will arrange to have the defendant return for his court appearances. He is not due to be sent overseas, since he has just returned from Viet Nam. Capt.   further stated that if this Court ordered that the relator not leave the confines of the City of New

York, the Army would arrange to station him here. Mr.   has previously been convicted of being a youthful offender, but, on information and belief, he never showed any propensity to avoid the orders of the court or to fail to appear in that proceeding.

8.   vehemently denies guilt of the charges against him. He does not wish to flee the jurisdiction, but rather to stay and establish his innocence. The events at issue in this case occurred in   , when the officer tried to have the relator and others leave the park, and an altercation ensued. The officer subsequently shot   twice, once through the body and once in the leg. He then shot a co-defendant,   , who is now free on $2500 bail. He has arrested both   and   , and on   , 1969, he arrested in court one   , a bystander at the altercation and a friend of the defendant's family. It is submitted that the circumstances of this case raise serious issues as to the guilt or innocence of the defendant.

9. On information and belief, the present bail of   is beyond the means of the relator's family. His mother and her family are supported by welfare payments. The present bail acts solely as a means of retaining the relator in jail, and punishing him without trial.

10. No court or judge of the United States Government has exclusive jurisdiction to order   released.

11. No previous application for the relief requested herein has been made.

WHEREFORE, your petitioner prays that an order issue, reducing the bail heretofore fixed to the sum of

STATE OF NEW YORK)
COUNTY OF NEW YORK) ss.:

                  ,   , being duly sworn, deposes and says that he is the petitioner in this proceeding, that he has read the foregoing petition, and the same is true to his knowledge except for those portions alleged to be on information and belief, and as to those, he believes them to be true.

Sworn to before me this
    day of   , 1970.

                                        Petitioner

163

Form 11—JUDICIAL SUBPOENA DUCES TECUM

CRIMINAL COURT OF THE CITY OF NEW YORK
COUNTY OF NEW YORK

Index No.

Calendar No.

PEOPLE OF THE STATE OF NEW YORK
—against—

Defendant

JUDICIAL
SUBPOENA
DUCES TECUM

TO: POLICE DEPARTMENT, CITY OF NEW YORK

GREETINGS:

WE COMMAND YOU, that all business and excuses being laid aside, you and each of you appear and attend before Part   , Criminal Court of the City of New York, County of New York, 100 Centre Street, New York, New York on the   day of   , 19   at 9:30 A.M., and at any recessed or adjourned date, to give testimony in this action on the part of the defendant and that you bring with you and produce at the time and place aforesaid, all records concerning the arrest and detention of   on   , 1970, at   , by officer   , shield #   or any other officer, including records entitled UF 61, DD5, UF 49, UF 4, UF 250, and all other written reports and photographs now in your custody, and all other evidences and writings, which you have in your custody or power, concerning the above.

Failure to comply with this subpoena is punishable as a contempt of Court and shall make you liable to the person on whose behalf this subpoena was issued for a penalty not to exceed fifty dollars and all damages sustained by reasons of your failure to comply.

WITNESS, Honorable   ,   one of the judges of said Court at 100 Centre Street, the   day of   ,   , 1970.

J.C.C.

164

FORM 12 — NOTICE OF APPEAL

CRIMINAL COURT OF THE CITY OF NEW YORK
COUNTY OF NEW YORK

PEOPLE OF THE STATE OF NEW YORK,
                    , Plaintiff-respondent,
        —against—
                    , Defendant-appellant.

SIRS:

PLEASE TAKE NOTICE that the above-named defendant appellant hereby appeals to the Appellate Term of the Supreme Court of the State of New York, First Department, from the judgment of conviction rendered against him on , 1970 in Part 2B of the Criminal Court of the City of New York, County of New York, in which defendant was sentenced to three months in the New York City Correctional Institution for Men, and from each and every part of said judgment.

> Yours, etc.
> Attorney for defendant
> Address
> Telephone

TO: District Attorney, New York County
     Clerk of the Appellate Term; First Department

Form 13A — NOTICE OF MOTION FOR CERTIFICATE OF REASON-ABLE DOUBT

SUPREME COURT OF THE STATE OF NEW YORK
SPECIAL AND TRIAL TERM PART 30;
NEW YORK COUNTY

PEOPLE OF THE STATE OF NEW YORK,	NOTICE OF
, Plaintiff — Respondent,	MOTION
—against—	
, Defendant — Appellant.	Docket No.

SIRS:

PLEASE TAKE NOTICE that upon the annexed affirmation of duly affirmed on the day of 19 , and upon all the pleadings and proceedings heretofore had herein, the undersigned will move this Court at a Special and Trial Term Part 30 thereof, to be held at the Courthouse, 100 Centre Street, New York, New York, on the day of , 19 , at 10:00 A.M. or as soon thereafter as counsel can be heard, for an order granting defendant a certificate of reasonable doubt and admitting him to bail pursuant to the provisions of §§460.50 and 530.50 of the Criminal Procedure Law pending the determination of defendant's appeal from a judgment convicting him of violating §240.05 of the Penal Law, and for such other and further relief as to the Court may seem just and proper.

DATED: New York, N.Y.
       , 19

                    Yours, etc.,
                    Name of Attorney for Defendant
                    Address
                    Telephone

TO: Frank S. Hogan
       District Attorney
       100 Centre Street
       New York, N.Y.

       Clerk, Part 30
       Supreme Court
       New York County

FORM 13B — AFFIRMATION IN SUPPORT OF MOTION FOR CERTIFICATE OF REASONABLE DOUBT
CAPTION
STATE OF NEW YORK)
COUNTY OF NEW YORK) ss.:

, an attorney at law duly licensed to practice in the courts of the State of New York, hereby affirms the following under penalties of perjury:

1. I am an attorney associated with the attorney of record for the above-named defendant and I am fully familiar with the facts and circumstances of this case. I make this affirmation in support of the annexed motion for a certificate of reasonable doubt and an order admitting defendant to bail pending his appeal.

2. Defendant and one other person were arrested on   , in the City, County and State of New York, and defendant was charged with incitement to riot and riot in the second degree, and the other person was charged with conspiracy to incite riot.

3. On   and   defendant was tried before a three-judge bench consisting of Hon.   , Hon.   , and Hon.   , in Part 2B of the Criminal Court of the City of New York, County of New York. After trial, the person arrested with the defendant was acquitted, defendant was acquitted of inciting to riot, and convicted of riot in the second degree. On   , defendant was sentenced to three months in the New York City Correctional Institution for Men.

4. A Notice of Appeal for said judgment of conviction was duly filed and served on   . The appeal is based upon the following grounds:

On July 26, 1968, Hon.   , one of the judges of the Criminal Court of the City of New York, denied defendant's timely motion for a jury trial. There are at present, conflicting decisions on the question of the right to a jury trial in misdemeanor cases. In the case of *People v. Marvin Puryear* Judge Jack Rosenberg, in an opinion handed down on September 11, 1968, ruled that a person accused of committing a class A misdemeanor is entitled to a jury trial. On the other hand, Judges
    ,   and others have been denying requests for juries made by persons accused of misdemeanors. There have been no rulings by superior courts in New York on this issue since the Supreme Court's decision in the case of *Duncan v. Louisiana*, 391 U.S., 145 (1968), in which the Supreme Court ruled that an accused was entitled to a jury trial in all "serious" cases, with the definition of the word "serious" left to the states.

The second basis for appeal is that defendant was convicted of riot in the second degree, which requires that the defendant be guilty of "violent and tumultuous conduct." At the trial the testimony of the police officers related almost entirely to mere statements made by the defendant which tended to show incitement to riot but which do not constitute riot. Nevertheless, the Court found that the evidence was insufficient to convict the defendant of incitement to riot but was sufficient to find the defendant guilty of riot. There was not sufficient evidence to convict the defendant of riot.

5. No previous application has been made for the relief requested herein.

WHEREFORE, your deponent respectfully requests that the court grant a certificate stating that in the opinion of the court there is a reasonable doubt that the judgment of conviction should stand, and ordering that the defendant be admitted to bail in the sum of $1.00 pending his appeal.

Dated: New York, New York
      , 19

Form 13C — ORDER GRANTING CERTIFICATE OF REASONABLE DOUBT

	At a Special Term of the Supreme Court of the State of New York, held in and for the County of New York, at

PRESENT:

HONORABLE

JUSTICE

At a Special Term of the
Supreme Court of the State
of New York, held in and for
the County of New York, at
the Courthouse, 100 Centre
Street, City, County and
State of New York on the
day of   ,
19

THE PEOPLE OF THE STATE OF NEW YORK

               RESPONDENT,   ORDER

     —against—

               DEFENDANT-APPELLANT

The appellant above named,   , having been convicted in the Criminal Court of the City of New York, County of New York, Part 2B3 thereof, of the crime of violating Section 240.05 of the Penal Law, riot in the second degree, on the   day of   , 19   , and having duly appealed from said judgment of conviction to the Supreme Court, Appellate Term, First Judicial Department, and having moved before this court for a certificate that in its opinion there is reasonable doubt whether such judgment of conviction should stand, and for an order admitting the defendant to bail pending the determination of the aforesaid appeal, and said motion having duly come to be heard on the   day of   ,   , 19   , and   , attorney for appellant, having submitted an affidavit in support of said motion, and Hon. Frank S. Hogan, District Attorney of New York County, by   , Assistant District Attorney, having appeared for the respondent herein and not opposing the certificate of reasonable doubt and to the Order fixing bail, and due deliberation having been had thereon,

Now, upon reading and filing the Notice of Motion, dated the   day of   ,   19   ,   and   the   affirmation   of   , Esq., duly affirmed the   day of   , 19   , and upon all the proceedings heretofore had herein, it is

ORDERED, that the motion be and the same hereby is granted, and it is

CERTIFIED, that in the opinion of this Court there is reasonable doubt whether the judgment of conviction rendered against the appellant in the Criminal Court of the City of New York, County of New York, Part 2B3 thereof, on the   day of   , 19   should stand in that there was a denial of jury trial, and the judgment of the conviction is against the law, and the evidence and the weight of the evidence present questions of law and fact which should be reviewed by an Appellate Tribunal, and it is

ORDERED, that the appellant,   , be admitted to bail pending the determination of the appeal duly taken herein upon furnishing a proper undertaking in the amount of one dollar which shall be considered bail pending the determination of the appeal from the judgment of conviction herein, and it is

ORDERED, the Warden of the House of Detention for Men, in the County of New York, or any other Warden having custody of the said   appellant, upon being served with a certified copy of this order and proof that bail has been furnished shall forthwith release the said   from imprisonment.

ENTER:

J.S.C.

170

FORM 14 — MOTION FOR NEW TRIAL and ORDER GRANTING NEW TRIAL

Adapt Form 6 for a NOTICE OF MOTION FOR NEW TRIAL

CAPTION: AFFIDAVIT IN SUPPORT OF MOTION FOR NEW TRIAL

STATE OF NEW YORK)

COUNTY OF NEW YORK) ss.:

, being duly sworn, deposes and says:

1. I am the defendant in the above-entitled action and I make this affidavit in support of my annexed motion for a new trial on the grounds that there exists newly discovered evidence which was discovered subsequent to the trial and which warrants a new trial.

2. On   , 19   , at approximately 11:00 P.M., on the complaint of   , I was arrested and charged with Burglary, Attempted Rape, and Assault in the third degree. Subsequently the first two charges were dropped and on Monday,   , 19   , I was tried in Part 2B3 of this court on the charge of assault in the third degree and after trial found guilty. An investigation and sentence was ordered and I am scheduled to be sentenced on   , 19   .

3. At the trial the complaining witness testified that I struck her about her face and that as a result, she suffered bruises and abrasions on her face which she claimed were clearly visible. She also testified that she did not see a physician and that she did not have pictures of her condition taken after the alleged crime.

4. I testified at the trial that I never laid a hand on her, that we had been out on a date that evening and that I had simply brought her home, and that she never had any visible injuries of any kind on her face or any other part of her body. After the trial, which lasted approximately 20 minutes, I was convicted of assault in the third degree.

5. At my arraignment on   , 19   , I was represented by a Legal Aid attorney, whose name I did not write down, who observed that the complaining witness did not have any visible injuries on her person. Prior to the trial I did not know this witness' name or how I could find him. Two days after the trial I met him by chance near the Courthouse and informed him of what had taken place. He then informed me that his name is   , that he remembers my arraignment and that the complaining witness did not have any visible injuries on her person at that time. He could act as a witness in my behalf at a new trial.

6. I am   years of age, have never previously been arrested, and I am presently an alien desirous of citizenship in the United States. Accordingly my conviction in this matter is of great importance to me since it could result in my deportation or in my being denied citizenship.

7. I am absolutely convinced and I do hereby solemnly swear that I am

not guilty of any crimes whatsoever against this complaining witness and I believe that if I am permitted to introduce the above-described newly discovered evidence at a new trial I will be found not guilty.

WHEREFORE, your deponent respectfully requests than an order be made and entered setting aside the conviction in this matter and directing that a new trial be held at any date convenient to the court, and for such other and further relief as to the court may seem just and proper.

At a Trial Term of the
Criminal Court of the City of
New York held in and for the
County of New York at the
County Courthouse located
at 100 Centre Street in the
City, County and State of
PRESENT: New York, on the day of
   Hon.   , 19   .
           JUDGE

CRIMINAL COURT OF THE CITY OF NEW YORK
COUNTY OF NEW YORK

PEOPLE OF THE STATE OF NEW YORK   ORDER GRANTING
       —against—   NEW TRIAL
                 , Defendant   DOCKET NO.

Upon reading and filing the notice of motion herein dated the   day
of   , 19   , the affidavit of   ,
sworn to the   day of   19   , and upon all the prior
proceedings had herein, and after hearing oral argument by the defendant
appearing pro se and by the District Attorney of New York County in
opposition thereto, and it appearing to the satisfaction of this court that
the newly discovered evidence is of such a character as in the interests of
justice requires that the defendant   be
granted a new trial, now, on motion of   ,
appearing pro se, it is
   ORDERED that said motion be and the same hereby is in all respects
granted, and it is further
   ORDERED that the conviction of the above defendant
               be and the same hereby is set aside, a new trial
of said defendant is hereby ordered and the said action is hereby placed
on the trial calendar of this court for the   day of   ,
19   , for trial.

                  ENTER:

                     J.C.C.

FORM 15 — MOTION TO INSPECT GRAND JURY MINUTES AND DISMISS INDICTMENT (OR INFORMATION).

Adapt Form 6 for a NOTICE OF MOTION TO INSPECT GRAND JURY MINUTES AND DISMISS INDICTMENT

CAPTION—AFFIDAVIT IN SUPPORT OF MOTION TO INSPECT GRAND JURY MINUTES AND DISMISS INDICTMENT

STATE OF NEW YORK)
COUNTY OF NEW YORK) ss.:

affirms under the penalties of perjury:

1. I am an attorney admitted to the Bar of this Court, with offices at   , and I make this affidavit in support of defendant's motion to examine the Grand Jury minutes.

2. The first ground of the present motion relates to the first and second counts of the indictment herein, in which it is charged that the defendants conspired, under Count I, to commit a robbery, and under Count II, to commit murder. These two conspiracy counts are based entirely upon the testimony of one   .   , it appears, is not a police officer, but an informer who participated in the alleged conspiracy. There is, on information and belief, no corroboration for the conspiracy charges apart from this testimony of an accomplice. Such evidence would be insufficient by itself to support the indictment, and defendants submit that there is no, or not sufficient, corroboration as to these counts of the indictment.

3. The second ground of the present motion relates to the Third Count of the indictment, in which all defendants are charged with attempted murder by attempting to kill a detective with a sawed-off shotgun. In the affidavit in the Criminal Court (attached), it was charged that defendant   pointed said gun at the detective. On information and belief, there is no more proof than that, and the pointing of the gun alone does not and cannot constitute attempted murder. Although the indictment alleges an intent to kill the detective, on information and belief there is no proof of said intent. This is a most important point in the present case, because the charges herein are extremely serious, and the actions of defendants are alleged to have roots of a political nature. To add to the already serious conspiracy charges a charge of attempting to kill an officer is extraordinarily prejudicial to the defendants. It is essential that the defendants not have a charge such as attempted murder heaped unnecessarily on top of the other charges herein.

4. The third ground of the present motion relates to the seventh, eighth and ninth counts of the indictment. It is submitted that, on information and belief, the testimony in the ground jury shows that the defendants were arrested in an automobile coming off a highway into Man-

hattan. They never attempted any of the aforementioned crimes, because they never came close to the premises that it was alleged that they attempted to rob. Nothing that they did rises to the level of an attempt to commit robbery.

WHEREFORE, it is respectfully requested that an order be granted permitting the defendant to inspect the minutes of the Grand Jury.